To Kelly
Stick to your values
& you've going to make
a brilliant coach
Cheers
Jim

THE
CLARITY METHOD

Tap Into What Motivates Your Clients,
Your Colleagues, and You

TIM BROWNSON

TheClarityMethod™

GW00673712

For Helen.
This is why I spent so much
time locked away in my office.

TABLE OF CONTENTS

FOREWORD

"Values. Right up there with oxygen." When I wrote those words in my first book, *How to Be Brilliant,* I really believed I knew a thing or two about values.

How mistaken can one be?

Like many people, I was faced with a dilemma. I thought I knew what my values were. As a coach and trainer, I would encourage people to discover their own values. I'd stand on stage and give glib advice such as, "Decision making is easy – once you know your values."

The fact was, like many so many truths, you don't know what you don't know.

In my quest to be a better version of me, I'd listened to millions of minutes of audio programs, read hundreds of books and traveled thousands of miles to see the gurus. You know the ones: big teeth and bigger hype. They all made a difference, but still there was a nagging question gnawing in the back of my mind.

How do you help someone, even yourself, to genuinely understand, find, articulate and live their life based on their core values?

And then I met Tim Brownson.

When I say that I met Tim, I've never actually been in the same room as him since he lives more than 4,000 miles from me. Somehow we became friends and—this is the best bit—Tim has become my go-to coach on values.

He's rather good at other areas of coaching too but if you really want to understand values, Tim's the one person whom I confidently recommend to everyone.

I'd better explain why.

As you'll see throughout the pages of this book, Tim is a realist. You'll not see much advice along the lines of "Chant your wishes" or "Just send out a message to the universe and relax as the universe will always give you what you need." That's not Tim.

But at the same time he does have many magic-wand moments where something that could have taken you years to discover will become crystal clear in a few magical minutes.

And he's funny. Well, he thinks he's funny and that's a starting point. Tim's comfortable with saying how it really is. You'll find yourself smiling on every page and even, as I did, laughing out loud many times as you dive in. And you will dive in—but be careful.

As you read *The Clarity Method*, you'll feel tempted to skip the exercises and put off the tough questions. You'll confidently tell yourself you can come back to this exercise or test out that idea later. Don't.

Understanding something after you've read it is good. Doing something about it in that moment can change your life.

And if you're really going to use Tim's powerful ideas to teach, help, and support others, could you put your hand on your heart and tell me you'd feel comfortable advising someone to do something that you haven't done yourself?

Much of Tim's work is based on solid research. I've always admired how he appears to be at the cutting edge of the latest thinking, and even more so how he takes what can be complex models and makes them easy for simple folk like me to understand and use.

But where Tim's real skill and expertise comes from is the knowledge gained from the thousands of people he has coached and the hundreds of coaches he has taught to be better coaches.

The examples you will read are real—many from individuals who have experienced their own life-changing transformations while being coached by Tim. Using The Clarity Method™, you will do the same. By educating yourself and helping others to really understand what motivates them, why they make the decisions they make, and how to live a fulfilled and happy life, you will be giving a gift that changes lives and lasts a lifetime.

Michael Heppell
Best-selling author of *Flip It*

Acknowledgments

I want to offer a massive thanks to all my clients. Without them and their brilliant hard work, determination, and feedback, this book could never have happened.

And, of course, we want to thank our newsletter and blog readers for keeping us on our toes. I know that when we get things wrong, you will point out the error of our ways but in a respectful way.

I would also like to thank Chris Gaskill, and Kate Di Cerbo for their invaluable help in transitioning from the first two iterations of *Aligning With Your Core Values* into what you have now, *The Clarity Method*. And also, a huge thanks to Angela Anderson and Kristi Anderson for help with editing, Dragan Bilic for the cover design and Leila Summers for keeping me on track.

"A leader will find it difficult to articulate a coherent vision unless it expresses his core values, his basic identity. One must first embark on the formidable journey of self-discovery in order to create a vision with authentic soul."

—Mihaly Csikszentmihalyi, author of Flow and leader in the Positive Psychology movement

THE CLARITY METHOD: INTRODUCTION

Many years ago, when I was about 10 or 11 years old, I was trying to fit in with some boys a year or so older than me. It was the beginning of my first year at a big, new school and I had few friends close to me because those of us who had moved up together had been split up across the entire lower form. As such, I was eager to please the other new boys in my class so I could feel included.

I had latched onto a group of about four boys and we were walking home from school one late afternoon. As was common practice, we stopped to go into a small convenience store that sold everything from fruit and vegetables to the more desirable candy. In those days, we all wore school uniforms and I had on a new blazer that was a bit too big for me, making me look a bit like Paddington Bear minus the marmalade sandwich under my hat.

I was wandering around the store ruing the fact that I didn't have any money to buy anything lovely and sweet, when suddenly I felt something heavy drop into the right-hand pocket of my blazer. I nervously looked down and could see an orange nestled neatly in the pocket.

I looked back up to see one of the other boys grinning at me. He put his finger to his lips and gently pushed me toward the door, obviously wanting me to leave with the 'free' orange.

I immediately felt sick with nerves. I'd never stolen anything in my life, and this didn't feel good at all. Neither did the thought of my trying to put the orange back and getting caught or telling the store owner that my new friend was attempting to encourage me to steal his produce.

I must have had guilt written all over my face because I was barely a half dozen paces through the door when I felt a large hand on my shoulder. I spun round hoping it was my friend but deep down knew it wasn't. My worst fears were realized as I faced an angry store owner who immediately thrust his hand into my pocket and pulled out the errant orange. I was so anxious, that I had to fight the urge to throw up all over the guy.

He brandished the *citrus reticulata* in front of my face and said, "What do you think you're doing with this? Are you a thief? I'm going to call your parents." I could barely talk, I was so frightened. My fear intensified as I saw my new friends walk off laughing, obviously not in the least bit concerned by my predicament.

To the best of my knowledge, that was the first time I was introduced to values. It was a chastening experience explaining to my parents why I'd done such a thing after they had been called to collect me. They felt let down but probably more importantly, I felt I'd let myself down to such an extent that I vowed I would never allow myself to get dragged into such behavior again.

I value honesty and integrity and I demonstrated neither. But equally, I value loyalty and friendship—even if in hindsight both were misplaced in that instance—and as such never told my mum and dad the true story until many years later. I felt the pull to be honest but I was conflicted because I didn't want to be the honest kid who had no friends. Nobody said life was easy, right?

Of course, I had no idea at that age what values were. I just knew something was badly amiss. It would be another thirty years or more before I'd fully understand their immense power when it comes to coaching others.

I was working with Jeff, an attorney who had come to me wanting help in creating a better work-life balance. He was already very successful, earned great money, had a gorgeous family he adored, and was on the path to becoming a partner in his law firm within three to five years.

The flip side was that he was working not far short of 100 hours per week because that is frequently what is expected for anybody aspiring to become a partner in a respected law firm.

I can remember thinking as we did the intake session, how on earth was I going to help him square the circle? He was one of the few people on earth who could genuinely claim there weren't enough hours in the day!

Most people tend to overestimate how many hours they work in a week, sometimes by large margins. They add up all the time they are at work but then forget to take away time spent doing things like trawling Facebook or any time-sucking social media site, reading the news, chatting with friends, eating lunch, or just staring into space and daydreaming about what they will spend the $100 million on with the winning Powerball ticket that's in their pocket.

Jeff wasn't one of those people. When he was at work, he had his head down and was pushing, pushing, pushing. He was a relentless workaholic determined to move from associate to partner at the law firm.

The reality is that there are only 168 hours in any week you care to mention, and, unless you're one of those extremely lucky people who can get by on minimal amounts of sleep, you're going to need about 50 of those for some shut-eye. That meant my client had about 18 hours per week to spend on everything not work-related.

Fewer than three hours per day for personal hygiene, relaxing, eating, exercise, spending family time—not to mention dealing with any of the unexpected events that life tends to throw at us from time to time—is not just taking things to the extreme but being reckless and setting yourself up to fail.

During the following session, we got into The Clarity Method™. I expected this to give me some insight as it almost always does but I wasn't prepared for what was about to happen.

The result of the process that I am shortly going to share with you was that his number-one value was Family, and his number-two value was Health.

I stood up and started to write the values down on the whiteboard on my office wall, and suddenly he started laughing. I turned around, as is the case when I hear somebody laughing, and started to do so myself. Only I had no idea what we were laughing at unless it was my handwriting, which was quite probable.

I managed to ask him what he was laughing at and he told me, "I don't really want to be partner, do I?" I responded, admittedly somewhat confused, "I don't know. What makes you say that?" He pointed to the whiteboard and said, "My wife and kids are the most important thing in the world to me, and my health is a close second. So why would I risk both of those chasing a job that will just entail more work?"

He went on to tell me that he could easily scale his work back to 60-70 hours per week if he was happy to stay an associate. And if this was frowned upon or not allowed, his résumé would get him a job at any small law firm where he could work on his own terms.

He stood up with a big grin on his face, thrust out his hand, and said, "I think we're done here." He was right; we were. He even refused to let me refund the money for the unused sessions he'd booked.

That's how powerful what you are about to learn can be. And whereas examples like that are not necessarily the norm, I rarely go through a week without having a breakthrough with a client using The Clarity Method™.

This process will not only help you but it will also allow you to help your clients, colleagues, or employees in your workplace become more effective. It will on occasion give you the kind of breakthroughs, like with my attorney client, that will take your breath away and have the people you are using The Clarity Method™ with thinking you're a genius—which I'm sure you are anyway.

I was once involved in a conversation in an online coaches' group after I had posted the question, "What gives you your biggest breakthroughs with your clients?"

The answers ranged from the rather scientifically dubious 'teaching them affirmations' to the expected 'helping them remove self-limiting beliefs,' on toward the more therapeutic 'using transactional analysis.'

In all, about 25 coaches responded—but only four pointed to core values work as the tool that helped them the most.

I found this both dispiriting and exciting: Dispiriting in that so many coaches were unaware of (or were ignoring) such a powerful tool, yet exciting because there is obviously an opportunity to spread the word and help coaches and leaders in the workplace become better at what they do.

As a Neuro-Linguistic Programming (NLP) Master Practitioner, I use those skills a lot, especially the linguistic side of NLP which can be incredibly powerful in a coaching environment. I'm also trained in hypnotherapy and although I don't practice hypnotherapy any more, I do use the language aspect of it to help clients too.

I use language patterns, clever questioning techniques (don't we all?), goal setting, reframing (known as *cognitive reappraisal* in therapy), and any number of other tools you care to think of.

None come close in importance to my work with core values and The Clarity Method™.

Imagine that by using the above tools, you have collected all the breakthroughs I have had with clients over the last decade and more, you put them in a bag, and then you place that bag on a set of scales.

Now imagine doing the same with The Clarity Method™ breakthroughs and gingerly lowering that rather large bag onto the other side of the scales.

My advice at this stage of what is quite frankly turning into a ridiculous metaphor would be to stand back, because when you let go of the values, they are probably going to catapult all the other tools back across the room and narrowly avoid killing a random pet or family member and demolishing your living room wall.

That is the importance of what you are about to learn in *The Clarity Method*, so let's get to it!

A WORD OF WARNING

As will become abundantly clear when you work through this book, values are highly personal things. You will find that every person you conduct this exercise with is different.

Since you have taken the trouble to buy *The Clarity Method*, I presume you are serious about helping others. Therefore, please do not be tempted to use this process on close friends and family members, even when practicing. Nothing good can come from it.

If you want to try this process out a few times before working with paying clients or employees—and I highly recommend you do—then find friends of friends or use Facebook, Twitter, or any other social media platform to ask for volunteers.

I tell a highly amusing (well it is now; at the time it was frightening!) story in my book, *How to Be Rich and Happy*, about the only time I ever did this with a married couple way back in 2006. That was an unmitigated disaster and I can assure you that I will never do it again. To cut a long story short, the wife—on seeing that her husband had the value of Family lower down on his list than she did—went what I can only describe as ballistic.

She started off by being verbally abusive and then when that failed to allow her to fully vent her ire, she got physical and hurled herself at her husband whilst at the same time aiming a knee at his nether regions.

She erroneously believed that because he didn't have Family at number one, then he must not love her and their kids as much as she did. But that isn't at all how values work. You carry scores of values with you and whereas there will be a certain hierarchy, that doesn't mean you can trample on some of them or dismiss them because they are not all at the top of the pile.

As will become abundantly clear as you work through the book, there are no right or wrong values, and a value sitting at number seven (or even number 15 if you bother to go that far), is still incredibly important to you or the person you are taking through The Clarity Method™.

You may well love your partner and family to bits (and I certainly hope you do) but trust me, they will have some values different from yours. Unless you know with absolute conviction that you can be very accepting, open-minded, and non-judgmental, there really is no need for you to know what they are.

Equally, if you are a parent, do not under any circumstances do this with your kids. First, their values are undoubtedly still being formed and as such, you are unlikely to get accurate results. But more importantly, it's highly probable that they will give you the answers they think you want to hear rather than what they really are. If you want to help them, get them their own coach—just not me.

I don't coach kids, and there are plenty of great coaches who specialize in helping young adults who are far more likely to benefit them than I would.

As I'm sure you realize, all names in the case studies have been changed.

"Your personal core values define who you are, and a company's core values ultimately define the company's character and brand."

—*Tony Hsieh, CEO of Zappos*

1

Why Are Values So Important?

Way back in 2008, I was working with a client from New York City. Here was a woman who had tragically lost her husband after a Taliban mortar attack took out the Humvee he was driving in Kandahar, Afghanistan.

I have no way of knowing if that was the reason she craved both stability and security so badly, but I suspect it certainly influenced her. To her, security meant financial security and even though she had received a 'death gratuity' from the US Army of $100,000 she was still almost obsessive about money.

After taking her through The Clarity Method™ and seeing both Security and Stability in her top five values, I had to drill down and get a better understanding of what she meant by these terms.

Note: As you will see later the book, I now get a client's definition or an example before I do the process but at this time I wasn't asking for either until after the process.

I asked her how much money she had now and how much she would need to feel secure. I presumed she had just short of the $100,000 paid to her by the government and as such wasn't at all prepared for her answer.

She had more than $300,000 in her checking account alone and a lot more tied up in stocks and shares—and her New York apartment was paid for. Unbeknownst to me, she had previously been a very well-paid and successful broker in the City.

I honestly cannot remember the figure she gave me that she said would allow her to feel secure, but it doesn't really matter because in situations like this it will never be enough. She already had enough money to live out her life without going hungry. Granted, maybe not in Manhattan's Upper West Side, but she could have lived like a queen in some parts of the world—maybe even in Queens.

As will become abundantly clear, I am dead against offering opinions on other people's values and even more against trying to change them. But I'm not convinced that either Security or Stability are real values and that's why I no longer include them on my sample worksheets.

Both Security and Stability can be tricky to work with as both are somewhat illusory. They can only ever be temporary and almost impossible to define. Neither value exists in nature; they are human constructs. I vacillate on whether to accept either from a client. Part of me wants to go with the flow but the other part knows that seeking a value that isn't truly achievable can lead to disappointment and unhappiness down the road.

However, the choice is yours whether you use these for yourself or accept them from somebody you're taking through The Clarity Method™. Or whether you encourage them to be relaxed about the fact that, as Benjamin Franklin pointed out, nothing is certain in life other than death and taxes—and taxes are debatable.

Understanding values is crucially important to you, your clients, and your employees or colleagues. I could say, "Trust me! I'm a life coach. I've been doing this stuff for donkey's years and they just are." But, I'm sure you're looking for a bit more substance than that, so let's take a closer look.

You may remember that in November of 2008 we had a presidential election in the United States. Not only was it the first time an African American was running for the White House but just as importantly in many respects, it was the first general election fought with the aid of social media. And, in particular, Facebook and Twitter.

This isn't the time nor place to explain how Barack Obama (or, more accurately, Obama's campaign managers) severely dented John McCain's chances by clinically utilizing social media and social networking. But, they did, and it probably won them the election.

What was even more fascinating, at least from a coaching and people-watching perspective, was how thousands of people who had gotten to know (and often like) each other through social networking over the previous months and years suddenly interacted with one another in a totally different manner. In many cases, idle banter, posting motivational quotes, and sharing videos of cute kittens on skateboards deteriorated rapidly into name-calling, unfriending, and even rather alarmingly, threats of physical violence.

What on earth had gone wrong?

Why do you think suddenly being aware of someone's political affiliations could cause such a change in people's attitude toward one another?

Values, that's why.

I don't want to get lambasted for my inappropriate use of language when it is so crucial to what we do as coaches and to good communication in general, but I'll risk it on this one occasion. What took place in the lead-up to the election was nothing short of social networking carnage.

People who had previously been getting on famously were suddenly declaring each other idiots, Nazis, libtards, and morons—and, in my case, I was told in one rather amusing exchange that I was a "Queen-loving Limey %&^*& that should %$#& off back from where I came." And by the way, I added the asterisks. She neglected to do so. Nice, eh?

The reality is that nothing had changed in the online relationships between people who had been previously fine with one another. They still liked idle banter, motivational quotes, and of course, cute kitties sliding down a bobsled run.

Except, that is, one crucial thing.

People's most important core values had risen to the surface for the entire world to see.

When you see the core values of an individual, you are effectively viewing his or her identity, and you are almost getting a window into his or her soul. I'm not a woo-woo kind of coach and I have no clue as to whether souls really exist, but I am only half joking when I say that. Why? Because that is the immense power of values and what they tell you about another person.

Core values are the things that people will, and sometimes do, die for. Ask a group of soldiers fighting in a conflict why they are doing so. Once you get past the ones who shrug their shoulders and reply, "I have absolutely no idea. I just want to go home," you will be bombarded by reasons that are value-based. I'm fairly confident that my client's husband didn't head off for his ill-fated mission because the money was good, and he just wanted to kill a few random strangers. No, he did it because he believed he was fighting for not just his freedom but also that of millions of his compatriots and our allies.

You could ask an ISIS or any extreme terrorist organization member the same question, though I don't advise it, and you will also get answers based upon values. They're just different values.

Whether you know it or not, the reason you're a coach or leader at work (CEO, manager, HR director, etc.) is because of your core values. I could make a fairly accurate guess as to what at least some of your values are just based on the fact that you're reading this book and looking to help people maximize their potential.

You almost certainly value legacy, significance, empathy, compassion, learning, and wisdom. I'm not necessarily saying they are your top values, but to some extent you will embrace most, if not all, of them.

Bearing that in mind, even though the events leading up to the 2008 election were somewhat sad, they were still highly predictable and nothing as childish as they might at first have seemed to many people.

Note: As I rewrite this book in early 2018, we have seen the same thing happen all over again, only this time it has been even more intensified and unpleasant. Rather than the election bringing an end to things, it seems more like it's been a springboard to create even more divisive behavior based upon values.

I have written about topics as diverse as God, health care, the Law of Attraction, and patriotism for my blog and they nearly always generate more comments and debate than if I talk about general coaching or self-development matters. I'm sure that if you write a blog or plan on doing so, you will see the same types of responses.

The reason for this is because people have values that are heavily invested in the former topics. As a coach or manager who coaches your employees, you probably have a strong opinion on coaching. Even so, I doubt very much you will rank the importance of coaching higher than that of health care, poverty, corruption, or war.

And even if we were to disagree with each other on whether *Your Brain at Work* or *Man's Search for Meaning* is the better self-development book, it's highly unlikely (I hope) that you'd want to maim or kill me to drive home your point.

When I wrote a post entitled "The 20 Greatest Self-Development Books of All Time," I literally did not receive one single death threat—or even a promise that I would be tarred and feathered. Sure, posts like that can create some spirited debate but by and large it's superficial and good humored.

Values are the antithesis of superficial and people will go to great lengths to make theirs known to others in an attempt to impose them. On more than one occasion, I have had aggressive and even threatening emails or comments on my blog from people who don't like my world view.

Values are crucially important because they drive your behavior from the moment you get out of bed in the morning to the moment you fall back to sleep in the evening. They should, if you are to make good ones, underpin all your major decisions, and many of your minor ones too.

Not knowing what your own values are can be problematic at best and crippling at worst, leading to a certain uneasiness, procrastination, unhappiness, and even anxiety. The Clarity Method™ can help remove that.

Not knowing your client's values, or those of people you are looking to motivate, is an entirely different story because that means you don't really understand them and what motivates them. In essence, you're playing a guessing game as to how best coach and motivate them.

I do understand that in its purest form you can adopt co-active or solution- focused coaching methods without knowing somebody at all, never mind their values. However, it does make it harder, and where's the point in that? I don't think I could coach nearly as effectively without understanding my clients' values because they explain many behaviors and are signposts to a happier and more fulfilling life.

Also, when coaching, it is our job to step onto our clients' map of the world and not ask them to meet us in the middle, or heaven forbid, see things as we do.

As such, not knowing their core values means we could at times be working parallel with them all the time and acting as little more than a very enthusiastic cheerleader. That's nice, but they can outsource cheerleading for $10 an hour and that kind of encouragement doesn't require a great deal of skill.

But worry not, because by the end of this book you will not only know what your values are but be in a position to use them to help others get better results in their lives.

"Does coaching work? Yes. Good coaches provide a truly important service. They tell you the truth when no one else will."

—*Jack Welch, former CEO of General Electric*

2

So, What Exactly Is A Value?

At the time of writing, Wikipedia defines a value system thusly: A value system is a set of consistent ethic values (more specifically the personal and cultural values) and measures used for the purpose of ethical or ideological integrity.

I can't say I disagree with any of that. Then again, I'm not sure what it really tells us because we are the ones left to define what is ethical and what demonstrates integrity. They're subjective terms and mean different things to different people based on, not unsurprisingly enough, the values and beliefs the person holds. Not only that but ethics and integrity can be values in and of themselves.

Confusing stuff, right?

Do you remember prior to us all having hi-def television, watching an advert on TV on your old low-def set extolling the virtues of a swanky new super cool, ultra-flat, hi-def 3D TV that cost more than your first house?

It was a frustrating experience because it didn't make any difference what they showed you or how amazing they told you the picture was. You were still looking at a low-def 2D picture. No matter how they blurred round the image to make it look clearer, we couldn't ever really see what they were trying to demonstrate. It was a ruse.

To a certain extent, the same goes for values.

When we look at a situation and decide whether it is right or wrong, good or bad, positive or negative, we do so through the filter of the values and beliefs we already hold, and there is no way of entirely getting round that.

It's like going shopping for a new shirt and wearing sunglasses with green lenses. Sure, you may come home with something that will wow your friends, but you're equally likely to have bought something that looks like your cat threw up on it.

A few years ago, I was questioned by one of my readers after I declared there are no right or wrong values, just values that are right or wrong for the individual.

Surely, she argued (and not unreasonably), things like murder are always wrong.

To begin with, murder isn't really a value because the value would be what the person was looking to achieve through committing the act of murder.

I don't want to dwell too much on this but let's suppose a battered housewife were to murder her husband. It could be for any number of reasons that are value-driven:

Perhaps she is scared to leave her home for fear of what he might do and is chasing freedom.

Or perhaps it is peace she is seeking and to calm her anxious mind.

Or it could even be that her life is filled with tumult and fear and she is seeking a certain level of stability.

And there are lots of examples where it's not so easy to say murder is wrong:

Is the man who returns home to find an intruder raping his wife wrong to shoot him?

What about the soldier who has been sent into war and is coming under enemy fire? Is he wrong to shoot back?

And what about the police officer who shoots an unarmed thief in the back who won't stop running? Is he in the wrong?

My guess is you replied something like this:

Of course not!

Or

Er, what? I don't know, give me more information. Maybe, maybe not.

Or maybe you didn't need more information because you have a belief that the police should never be unloading their weapons unless they are fired upon.

On the flip side, perhaps you think the police should have every right to shoot a suspected felon if they won't stop fleeing, irrespective of whether they are being directly threatening.

You have opinions on what you believe to be right or wrong and that's fine. Just understand that these opinions are based on your beliefs and values that create your world view and nothing else. And I do mean nothing else.

One of the things that separates us from animals is our belief in right and wrong. We believe that there is right and wrong, good and evil. Animals, not so much.

Trust me, there's never been a lion roaming the Serengeti racked with guilt about orphaning some buffalo calves after snacking on their mum. And there has never been a crocodile muttering five Hail Mary's after being tempted to eat a much smaller baby crocodile for brunch when the buffaloes never showed at the watering hole and he was a bit peckish.

Would you admonish the lion and the crocodile for being naughty, albeit it from a safe distance?

Of course not, because you understand there is no right or wrong or good or evil in nature. They are merely human constructs.

I realize I'm stripping this down to the bare bones, a bit like the lion did with the buffalo, and being very literal. There must be some societal values agreed upon, even if it's only tacitly. Otherwise, law and order would break down.

If you really want to understand The Clarity Method™ and maximize core values with your clients and the people you are coaching, it's critical to get your head round this.

If you disagree, then you will always be coming from a position that your values are more important than other people's.

As a coach and leader, that approach is going to create a lot of dissonance between you and the people you are trying to help.

It makes building rapport exponentially harder and prevents you from seeing their true picture.

Of course, I don't think murder is right. I also don't think lots of other things are right, such as: harming others, animal cruelty, homophobia, racism, fundamentalism, or stealing oranges. But that's only my opinion based on my values and world view. It doesn't make murder right, no matter how much you or anybody else agrees. Or even how much I want it to be so.

There is no 'how it is,' only 'how it is *for you*.' Or as the Bard so eloquently put it in Hamlet, "There is nothing either good or bad but thinking makes it so."

When it comes to beliefs, there is absolutely no correlation whatsoever between how much you believe something to be true and it being true. In fact, the opposite can often be true.

In March of 2011, doomsday 'prophet' Harold Camping predicted that Jesus Christ would return to Earth on May 21st of that year, and the Rapture would get underway with all non-believers facing a grim future of fire, brimstone, and long lectures in a hot room from a man with a pointy tail.

Hundreds of thousands of people believed Camping and prepared themselves for a journey going either one of two ways. And the reason they did this is because they shared many core values and beliefs with Camping.

As you now know, because you're reading this book, things didn't pan out quite as Harold envisioned. However, not to be deterred by his lack of initial success (he had once before suggested such a thing would happen), he did some quick calculations and admitted he'd got it wrong and it was going to be October 21st after all.

You would think that this time nobody would have listened to him, but sadly you'd be wrong, and hundreds did. Fortunately for all of us, after nothing happened that time either, Harold did the world a favor and retired from prophesying.

Your core values (like the aforementioned beliefs) are determined and shaped over many years almost entirely by external stimuli. In fact, they're not even really your own values. You've simply acquired them through exposure to a million and one different things during your life. Babies aren't born with values any more than they are born with a belief system.

Actually, scratch that, because even though it's almost true it's a tad misleading. As Abraham Maslow demonstrated with his hierarchy of needs, all humans are born with certain inherent needs like air, food, water, shelter, etc. On top of that, we now know the crucial importance of connection as well as good health when we are growing up. So, in a sense, we are born with certain values that help us survive and thrive. We'll talk more about this later when we look at inherent values.

Your values have been shaped and influenced by countless things, including your family (or lack thereof), your friends, television, politicians, church leaders, cultural influences, books you have read, incidents (both positive and negative) you've seen or been involved in, the country you were born in, conversations you have had, schools you attended, and much more.

You can see the infinite amount of permutations—and why in more than 12 years of full-time coaching at the time of this writing, I've never had two clients with the same top 3 values as mine.

And before you presume that's because I'm a bit weird, it really isn't. Well okay, I may be a bit weird but my values aren't. To prove it, here they are:

Peace

Freedom

Integrity

Note: Interestingly, I had somebody who I was teaching The Clarity Method™ to take me back through the process this week. Eight years on from originally undertaking the process, my values were: Peace, Humor, and Freedom—with Integrity coming in at number four. Previously, number four had been Humor, so it was very interesting to see things were very much as they were.

I happen to like those values and think they're cool, but apparently not one single client of mine agrees completely. Because if they did, they'd have them too and, as I said, that's never happened.

Other than situationally and culturally, our values tend to shift less the older we get. As with our beliefs, we all have a tendency to look for information to cement the values we already possess and filter out information to the contrary.

That's the reason why so few Republicans would ever watch a Michael Moore movie other than with the intention of pouring scorn on it. Equally, it's why most Democrats would rather listen to six hours of white noise than "The Rush Limbaugh Show."

To drive home this point, there is a fascinating story in the excellent book *Mistakes Were Made (But Not by Me)* by Carol Tavris and Elliot Aronson.

When some Palestinians were shown recommendations for the peace process that they were told came from the Israelis, they dismissed them out of hand. Similarly, when Israelis were shown supposed Palestinian ideas for peace, they turned them down.

What neither group knew was that the proposals had actually been drawn up by members of their own social group and not by the side they saw as the opposition.

In other words, they had made up their mind before they had even read the proposals and were simply scanning for evidence to support the decision they had already made. In psychology, this is a cognitive bias called *confirmation bias*, and it involves the brain seeking information to support pre-held beliefs and opinions.

We are all prey to confirmation bias to a certain extent but it can sometimes help or hinder us. If you have a belief that you suck as a coach or manager (and hopefully you don't hold such a pernicious belief), then when something doesn't go according to plan, you are highly likely to ruminate on it and feel even worse.

Your brain has decided you're not good enough and as such it will search for evidence to support the belief. When it finds some, it will latch onto it with a "Ha! I knew I was right. I knew I wasn't good enough and that tiny mistake I made six years ago just goes to prove it."

To do otherwise creates cognitive dissonance, which is the unpleasant feeling we get when we try to hold two contradictory beliefs at the same time. Under such circumstances, if the brain is left unattended it will always look to support the stronger belief because it's much easier and your grey matter very much likes things to be easy.

Your brain is very greedy when it comes to energy, requiring between 20% and 25% of your daily supply in the form of glucose and oxygen. New thoughts require a lot more energy.

This is the reason why you can start a new job and be exhausted at the end of the day even though you've done little work.

Your brain has had to build a lot of new neural connections such as where you park, how to get from your office to the bathroom, learning the names of your new colleagues, how you access the company intranet and not forgetting to put covers on all reports.

Those kinds of things would have required next to zero mental exertion at your previous job because the thoughts would be grooved, filed away under "I got dat!" (probably) at a subconscious level. As such, they would require little input from your conscious mind which is the part that uses the bulk of your energy.

It's highly unlikely you will suddenly forget where the bathroom is once you have created that neural map, or remember how to get home if you have made that drive more than a few times. If you have ever moved home and then inadvertently found yourself on the driveway of your old home after work, you can say a big thank you to your well-grooved cranial highway for making you look foolish.

Anyway, detour over. Let's get back to confirmation bias so we can start to use it to our advantage. In the previous example of a mistake from six years ago, if instead of thinking, "Ha! I knew I was right. I knew I wasn't good enough," we opted for something like, "Wow, that is unusual. I very rarely make mistakes like that. In fact, I can think of at least 50 or more coaching sessions where I nailed it," and then we go on to mentally recount the successes, we can retain our self-esteem and confidence, and make it exponentially more likely that confirmation bias can work in our favor next time.

Neuroscientist and Buddhist teacher Rick Hanson in his book *Hardwiring Happiness* calls the act of remembering positive events like this and allowing the positive feelings that naturally arise 'taking in the good.' He goes on to say that repeatedly engaging in this process can not only allow us to be more relaxed about negative events, but significantly improve our happiness levels.

Although our values and beliefs don't tend to shift regularly, things can change radically under certain (and often traumatic) circumstances.

Suppose you've never had trust as a main value, and you come home early from work one day to find your partner in bed with your best friend. Do you think trust would suddenly find its way into your most important values?

I would say there is a better-than-even chance that trust would come crashing into the list of your most important values—and that infidelity would similarly become high on your list of anti-values. (More about anti-values later, but broadly speaking they are emotions, actions, and feelings that are anathema to you.)

Speaking of which, I don't ever remember a client having Infidelity as an anti-value who had not been through a relationship that went sour or having had parents who split up because of an extramarital affair.

Similarly, if health was something you took for granted because you had always been fit and vibrant and then you get a serious medical diagnosis, there is a high probability that health will shoot up your values list.

I'm pretty sure that if you had conducted The Clarity Method™ on me when I was thirty years old, peace would be nowhere in sight. It wasn't until I got into meditation in my early forties that I realized the importance of internal peace to me. Prior to then, I'd been highly argumentative, loud, and occasionally boorish after a beer or two. Okay, so maybe I can slip into being like that now but I'm way more aware of how I react and able to respond accordingly.

Fortunately, though, extremes like the first two examples above are not the norm, and your values will tend to remain relatively stable once you get into your thirties and beyond.

"A company's values—what it stands for, what its people believe in—are crucial to its competitive success. Indeed, values drive the business."

—Robert Haas, Chairman and CEO, Levi Strauss & Company

3

When Values Collide

Have you ever argued vehemently with friends or family members about politics, religion, whether it's right to give money to homeless people, the troubles in the Middle East, or the morality of the death penalty?

For the most part, this is because you have conflicting values on those subjects.

That's the reason you simply cannot ever agree on certain topics no matter how much somebody tries to persuade you, or you try to convince them. Of course, you may well still carry on banging your head against the proverbial brick wall and trying to drive home your point but all that is likely to happen is the argument gets polarized and tempers flare.

I'm sure at some stage in your life you have gotten into a vehement debate with somebody and you have introduced some killer proof that demonstrates you're in the right. But instead of the other person relenting to your undoubted genius, they double down and ignore the new information. For the most part, it's not them being willfully ignorant but the fact that when the brain comes under attack like that, it can shut down access to higher reasoning. In such cases, back off because agreement is next to impossible no matter what happens.

That doesn't in any way mean you can't be in a strong and stable relationship or friendship with somebody who has different values. In fact, it can often be just the opposite, because under the right circumstances different values can encourage compromise and deeper understanding, presuming both parties want that and are prepared to listen with an open and non-judgmental mind. And yes, open-mindedness and being non-judgmental can indeed be core values.

That said, it's usually wise to know when agreement will never happen and leave well alone. I stopped talking politics with my dad years before he died because we were poles apart and every discussion ended up with us thinking the other was a complete imbecile who was blind to the reality of the situation.

It's the ultimate in arrogance to believe we have a handle on what values are right and wrong and that others only need to understand that our beliefs are correct. Yet that is pretty much how every serious argument, fight, and war starts out.

These are my values, they're better than your values, and if you cannot see that, then I am going to force them upon you for being so ignorant and uninformed.

How many conflicts both large and small could be summed up with the above phrase? Probably most of them.

It's also at the root of evangelical and fundamentalist behavior. Both require the person to have a heightened sense of their own values and a belief that it is their job to impose them upon people who aren't fortunate enough to be so enlightened.

Forgive the sarcasm at the end but it's something that I feel strongly about because here's the rub with values:

As I intimated above when I explained how you acquire your values, they are, largely speaking, an accident of birth. Therefore, to look down upon another person's or culture's values means you are effectively saying, "You were really dumb to be born in that country, to that family, and at that time in history."

Seriously, that is exactly what you would be implying if you were questioning another person's values. Fortunately, I'm sure you're wise enough to know that is misguided at best—and ridiculous, pompous, and arrogant at worst—and as a coach and leader you would never act in such a manner. I understand that many people with evangelical beliefs try to foist them on others with the best intentions and often with a desire to help but that desire is misguided.

As human beings, we are hardwired to generalize. We do this in order to make sense of the world. For example, if every time you are wanting to leave a room, you don't generalize that the 8'x4' piece of wood with a handle on one side and hinges on the other is probably the door, you would have a very frustrating time getting through your day.

Unfortunately, we also do this with people. We have a very strong tendency to create *us and them* groups in our mind, often based on shared values. This causes us—sometimes consciously, more frequently unconsciously—to look more favorably upon those people we think are like us and thus have similar values, and less so on those we think are different.

"Core values are the essential and enduring tenets of an organization. A small set of timeless guiding principles, core values require no external justification; they have intrinsic value and importance to those inside the organization."

—Jim Collins, author of From Good to Great: Why Some Companies Make the Leap...and Others Don't

4

Preparing the Client for a Value Elicitation

I t sounds a bit fancy but a value elicitation is simply the process of uncovering your clients' values. When I do the values exercise with my clients, there are three very distinct phases that I want to take them through: Preparation, Values Heirarchy, and Values Application.

Phase One is Preparation, which starts at the end of the previous session (usually the intake session). I want to get into values after I have done my intake session to get a deeper understanding of what I am dealing with before we dive into coaching.

After the first session, I set up the following one by explaining what core values are and why it's so crucial for the client to understand them. I emphasize that walking through The Clarity Method™ is probably going to be the most important session we do and that I want them to take the homework very seriously because it will lay the groundwork for our time spent together.

Even if you're not a coach and you are using this to bring the best out of a colleague, then I advise setting the agenda by saying something along the lines of:

"When we meet, we are going to get into some cool work around your core values. Values are so core and such a big part of our identity. Yet, many people go through their entire lives without ever understanding what their core values are. You have the opportunity to separate yourself from those people and truly understand what motivates you at the deepest level.

People will often ask themselves questions like, 'What goals can I set for myself?', 'How can I get promoted?', or 'How much money do I want to earn?' Rarely do they go the next level down by asking questions such as, 'Why is that so important to me?' or 'Can I still be happy if I don't achieve those things?'

I'm going to send you a sheet that has instructions on what to do between now and when we next speak. Please pay close attention to the instructions because it's important we get this right. Also, remember the sheet contains sample values and yours may be different from those on the list. In fact, I would be surprised if you didn't have a number of values that I haven't listed, as there are well in excess of 100 different values."

Note: In a coaching environment, I don't usually like the word 'why, and seldom use it because it's confrontational, problem-facing, and tends to make people defensive.

Think about it. If I asked you, "Why were you late for our coaching meeting?", I have asked you to defend yourself. I have sent you inside looking for a reason as to why you were late the same way as an angry parent would do with a child who brings home a poor report card and demands answers.

Imagine we are in a burning building together and I turn to you and say, "Why is this building on fire?" You're probably going to stare at me rather strangely before running for an exit without even so much as a fond farewell to the sizzling life coach.

I'm not saying that knowing the reason why something negative happened cannot have value because of course it can, just not as much as finding the solution to prevent it from happening again.

If you were late for a meeting with me, what if instead of my saying, "Why are you late?", I said, "What do we need to do differently to ensure you are on time when we are next due to meet?" Things are very different because that is a question looking for a solution, not an excuse or a defense.

That question maintains rapport and creates a puzzle to be solved. The human brain loves to solve problems and you are far more likely to come up with a solution than start on a rant about the traffic being a nightmare or being unable to get the kids off to school on time because young Jimmy ate your car keys.

If parents used this approach with kids, they would have way more success. Kids are by their very nature super curious. Asking them to help you solve a problem is exponentially more likely to get their buy-in than demanding to know why there is a B in the middle of a report card full of A's.

When working with values, however, using *why* can be very useful. I won't shy away from it because there is no real danger of breaking rapport and you're not really looking for a solution, per se, just a gut reaction.

You may be familiar with the TED Talk by Simon Sinek that went viral and proceeded to spawn a best-selling book called *Start With Why*. It was entirely based upon values and the way super successful, progressive companies drill down again and again and again to figure out what really matters to them as an organization.

Even though I go to great lengths to tell clients the list I send them is by no means exhaustive, I still occasionally get sixteen values back (8 from each side), all of which are on the sample sheets I have sent out.

If that happens to you, be very suspicious because odds are they are either careless or not engaged enough in the process and that's going to make it a lot harder for you to coach them effectively.

Van Halen lead singer David Lee Roth had quite the reputation in the late 1970s and early 1980s as a rock-and-roll diva, not least because of the extensive demands he put on concert venues with his legendary riders.

Riders are added to the contract between a band and performance venue stipulating additional requirements for the band to be able to play. Many of the riders are important and look at safety issues and the equipment that is to be made available, but others are less crucial.

Roth had his attorneys who drew up the rider drop in a random request— that a bowl of M&M's be placed in the dressing room—but there were to be no brown ones! They then positioned this in the middle of all the technical specifications.

This seemingly ridiculous request had nothing to do with the band hating brown M&M's. Nor did it have anything to do with rock-and-roll excess. Instead, it had a very specific purpose.

Van Halen was at the cutting edge of the huge theatrical-like music extravaganza and to put on such an event safely involved a lot of attention to detail. They had previously had an issue almost leading to the death of some of their road crew when there was an electrical problem due to carelessness on the part of the venue's staff.

Roth knew that if he got into the dressing room and there were either no M&M's, or there was a bowl containing brown ones, then they may have a problem because he knew the rider hadn't been read properly.

A client sending you eight core values and eight anti-values, all of which were on the sample sheet, almost certainly means they have rushed the process and you may have a commitment or engagement problem.

Of course, there is a remote chance that all their values are listed amongst the samples. But, seeing as there are well in excess of

100 values, it's about as likely as my waking tomorrow morning with a full head of hair, six-pack abs, and good looks to make Zeus weep with shame.

Fortunately, your client won't burst into flames because of a faulty amplifier or get trampled to death by a huge crowd, but you may end up with an inaccurate list of values and that's almost as bad.

Note: I have seen lists containing upward of 400 values. Personally, I think they are largely nonsense and contain words that aren't really values. If somebody tells you they have a value of Being Cool (and yes, I have seen that on a list), ask what being cool gives him or her. That answer is more likely to be a value because there is no value in being cool in and of itself.

Before I get back to the process, I just want to explain how you can potentially extract even more benefit from this exercise whether you are a professional coach, a manager, or a business owner.

You may be familiar with 'the four quadrants' made popular by Stephen Covey in his classic book, *The 7 Habits of Highly Effective People.*

Covey noticed that all human activity fits into one of four quadrants:

1. **Doing important work that is not urgent.**

2. **Doing important work that is urgent.**

3. **Doing unimportant work that is not urgent.**

4. **Doing unimportant that is urgent.**

When the book was first published in 1989, Covey suggested that far too many people spend a disproportionate amount of time in the *urgent but not important* quadrant and not enough in the *important but not urgent* section.

And that was before the advent of emails and the resulting deluge of information that many people now experience daily. Whether you are a coach or a manager, you will probably spend a good portion of your day trying to decide what is urgent and what can be put aside for another time.

But how much time do you spend deciding what is really important? That report may have a deadline of Friday at 5pm but is it going to cause anything more than mildly irritate your manager? You may have a dozen or more emails all asking you to respond at your soonest convenience but how many really require your immediate response?

One time when I was in sales, I went to see my manager. We had a huge open-plan office and she didn't see me approaching from behind. Just as I got to her shoulder, I saw her delete an unread email I had sent to her shortly before.

I asked her what she was doing, and she just looked sheepish and started laughing. Then she told me that she deleted almost every unsolicited email from people below her in the organization when it first hit her inbox. Her reasoning went that if it was truly important or urgent they would follow up with a second one. Whereas I'm not advocating that type of managerial approach, she did make an interesting point.

As the legendary actor John Wayne supposedly once said when a stagehand announced there was an urgent phone call for him, "Urgent for who? Me or the guy on the phone?"

When you are working with somebody else on their values, figuring out your own, or trying to set up business values, what quadrant do you think you're working in?

Exactly, important but not urgent.

In more than 12 years of doing values work with hundreds of people, I have never had anybody come to me needing an emergency value elicitation. Let me take that back. I did once have a woman who had an interview with the BBC in London call and ask if I could help her work out her values prior to the interview because she knew the job would entail a significant change of culture from her current position.

It's very easy to put off values work, especially on yourself and in the workplace because let's be honest, there will always more pressing priorities. But there will be little that is more important and will offer as much value going forward, which is why great companies take so much time on it.

You may think that as a coach or manager, values work is not applicable to you, and you would be wrong. If, as a life coach or company leader, you are out of alignment with your values, clients and employees will sniff you out a mile away. And not in a good way either.

As you saw earlier, one of my top values is Integrity, and that is why I am so transparent on my website. It's why I'm not averse to admitting I've had a bad day from time to time, and why I won't get involved in joint ventures unless it's for a product or service I would use myself and have researched. And it's why if you met me for a coffee or beer you wouldn't get any surprises, other than maybe I'm much more ruggedly handsome in real life than you ever imagined possible. [1]

My website at A Daring Adventure makes it obvious to anybody reading that I also value fun and humor and I am apt to swear a lot. So, guess what type of client I attract? Exactly! People who maybe don't want a coach who is stuffy and formal and who want to enjoy the process. To paraphrase John Lennon, my approach doesn't get me the most clients but it does get me the *best* clients—at least for me.

Of course, if you are a manager or small business owner and are using The Clarity Method™ with people in the workplace, then you must work with all different types of people. But—and it's a big but—everybody who works with you or for you should be on board with the company values.

To start The Clarity Method™ process, I send the list of sample values and a blank Excel document (see Addendum of sample values or visit www.claritymethod.com/bookstuff and ask clients to list eight values and eight anti-values. I used to ask them to email me eight from each side and then I'd fill in the matrix.

However, my clients would regularly send me more than eight, and there would be occasions when I'd receive 15 or more. Trying to deal with more than about 10 values considerably lengthens the process, so asking them to list their eight massively reduces the opportunity for them to send you a long list. Plus, it saves you the time of manually entering them into the spreadsheet.

Having said this, a client will sometimes add a couple extra values and I am okay with that. All I do is jot them down and then when the process is finished, slot them in (more on how I do this later).

Note: If you are incredibly observant, you may notice that there is no mention of 'happiness' on the sample sheet. That is deliberate. Not only is it not on the list but if a client adds it anyway, then I'll ask them for another core value and ignore happiness.

Knowing somebody wants to be happy doesn't tell me anything about them I don't already know—because everybody on the planet wants to be happy. In fact, I'd go as far to say it's everybody's number-one value. People may disagree and think other values are more important. However, what they really think at a subconscious level is that the values they think are more important are also likely (if they are in alignment with them) to make them happy. We will take another look at happiness and something I call inherent or global values later in the book.

On the flip side, and for reasons I have never quite nailed down, I will occasionally get a client who sends me fewer than eight values—although more often it's anti-values. If it's six or seven items, I may continue. Any less than that, though, and I really want to push them. Not being able to come up with eight anti-values when there are dozens is telling me something as a coach—and without further questioning, I don't know what that is.

Many years ago, when I was still a wet-behind-the-ears coach, I had a client who only sent back five anti-values. When I questioned her on this, she rather strangely refused to talk about it or add any more.

I continued and everything went fine with the core values side of things. But when we started on the anti-values, I could tell by her voice she was very agitated and upset. I stopped and asked her how she was feeling. To cut a long story short, she was a mess and I suggested we leave that side of the equation alone and just work with her core values.

Even though she was relieved, it was a mistake by yours truly. If you get a client who reacts to something so benign in such an extreme manner, then you have a problem. You may well have a client who needs therapy and not coaching, and you have a duty or care to tell them that, or at the very least suggest they talk to their primary care provider.

Footnote:

1. In the spirit of staying in alignment with my value of Integrity, the ruggedly handsome bit was a huge whopper of a lie.

"Your core values are the deeply held beliefs that authentically describe your soul."

—*John C. Maxwell, author of The 21 Irrefutable Laws of Leadership*

5

Understanding Your Clients' or Colleagues' Values

Phase Two is what we are about to do shortly, and that is to work out the Values Heirachy for your clients. It's cool knowing your own or a client's top eight values, but it's way cooler knowing which of those eight are the most important.

I want to stress again at this stage that whatever results you elicit are fantastic and you're definitely not looking to change them, but rather just get to know them a little better. Your values and your clients' values are what they are and they're just lovely, so give them a big hug without judgment or comment.

We all have dozens of values and there will be a certain hierarchy. However, that doesn't mean values that are lower down aren't important because they are. They are just not quite as important as those nearer the top. After the process, I regularly have clients say something along the lines of, "Wow, I can't believe that value is at the bottom." It's your job to assure them it's not at the bottom of anything other than their top eight, and the fact it has even made it on the list means it's still vitally important to them.

I limit this exercise to eight values simply because as I said earlier, each value you add after that makes the process significantly longer. However, there's no reason whatsoever why you cannot take this to 10 or 12 if you want. If you do, you will need to reformat the spreadsheet at the end of the book to allow you to order them efficiently.

Before you can move on to the value elicitation, there is something you must do with every single client, and that is get a total understanding of what each value means to your client. If you don't do this, then there is the potential for misunderstandings when you attach your interpretation of a word to your client's values.

And you do that by asking the following question, using Freedom as an example:

"What does freedom mean to you? Or, please give me an example of where you have seen freedom in action."

It could literally mean freedom of speech, financial freedom, freedom to travel, freedom to work independently, or even freedom to bear arms for that matter. You cannot afford to presume that your client's definition is the same as yours.

When I think of Freedom as a value that is personal to me, I automatically think of the freedom I gain from working for myself. I see clients when I want, I walk my dogs when I want, and—until some person stole my clubs out of my garage—I played golf (badly) when I wanted.

And what about Love, or Family, or Peace?

All these words have literal translations, and some will even have more than one literal translation, but equally they all mean different things to different people. When I think of the value Peace, I automatically think of internal peace; yet only this week I had a client with that value and to her it meant external peace. She had a job that involved dealing with customers, three kids, two dogs, and a seemingly demanding husband. It was no wonder she put so much store in finding literal external peace.

Now, you may think that if she could attain internal peace that her external circumstances would be less of a concern, but that's easier said than done in the real world. Of course, there are some enlightened souls, especially experienced meditators who can retain equanimity when enduring the slings and arrows of outrageous fortune, but most people have a tipping point.

It would be easy to look at a client's values and presume they have the same definition of a word or value as you do.

Don't do it!

Never presume that you know what the person you are working with means by any given value. In fact, tell yourself you are not even familiar with that word in the English language and as such you are forced to ask the client what he or she means:

What does Peace mean to you? Give me an example.

What does Freedom mean to you? Give me an example.

What does Humor mean to you? Give me an example.

I threw that last one in because I have a very strange sense of humor and often laugh at things that other people don't think are funny. It's said that "sarcasm is the lowest form of wit," yet I happen to think good sarcasm is incredibly funny and use it on a regular basis—much to the chagrin of friends and family.

It's crucial to get the person to specify as much as possible so you know exactly what you're working with. I have had all sorts of responses I wasn't expecting, such as the previously mentioned definition of peace. Without the upfront explanation, you can waste a lot of time and energy. Not just your time and energy either, but more importantly, that of the person you are coaching.

If you're working out your own business values, ask yourself what each value means to you and your employees, as well as what each can mean to your clients or customers. Write down the explanation and a time you have seen it in action.

What happened?

Why was it important to you?

How did it benefit your business and hopefully also the people you look to serve?

Get as clear on this as you can and take the time to write down what comes to mind rather than just ponder it. The act of writing it down makes it more real. To look at a word and say, "Yes, that is what I stand for and that is what I want other people to know that I stand for" is not the same as having some vague concept wandering the corridors of your mind unattended.

A QUICK WORD OF WARNING:

You are reading a book written by somebody who happens to think he knows a lot about values and how to use them in a coaching environment. I have conducted the process hundreds of times and these days I rarely get a hiccup.

Yet, as I was literally in the middle of writing the previous version of *The Clarity Method*, formerly called *Aligning With Your Core Values*, I got a huge wake-up call.

I was working with a male client and we were at the point where he had sent his values back to me and I had them ready to go on the call.

The values he sent me were as follows:

Family

Growth

Freedom

Integrity

Honesty

Competitive

Confidence

Passionate

As we just spoke about, I went down the list and asked for his interpretation of each word. In those days I didn't ask for an example. That is something I have started doing relatively recently and it can be incredibly useful.

Then, as we were about to start working out the hierarchy, I made some changes to the values to make them flow better.

Asking a client which is more important to him, Competitive or Passionate, sounds a bit clunky and doesn't flow as well, so I changed those two words to Competitiveness and Passion.

There is a saying in sales: "Parrot-phrase, don't paraphrase," and it means that when a salesperson is summing up a customer's reasons for buying, she should use the customer's exact words back, just like a well-trained parrot would.

As an example, when asking about a color, if the customer says she really likes lighter, vibrant colors, then that's the language the salesperson should use in summing up.

What she shouldn't do is go freestyle and say, "So let me get this right. You love colors like bright orange and yellow, right?"

That may not be what the customer meant at all and by saying that, the salesperson creates confusion and risks breaking rapport and even losing the sale. Meanwhile, the client is thinking, "I have no idea what the hell this lunatic is talking about because she obviously hasn't been listening to me. I'm outta here!"

It wasn't until I said to my client, "What's more important to you, Freedom or Competitiveness?" and he responded "Competitive," that I realized I'd screwed up and stopped the process for a moment to think it through.

Competitive and competitiveness are obviously closely linked, but they are not the same thing at all.

The former, an adjective and personal (associated), was telling me something about the client that Competitiveness, a noun, may not have been. The latter is more abstract and disassociated—a concept, if you will.

What I hadn't noticed was that he was waving a massive clue under my nose about his personality and I almost missed it. I apologized, explained I'd made a mistake, changed the words on my form, and continued.

I'm fairly sure this had never happened to me before, but I cannot be 100% sure and it may have. I am 100% sure it won't happen again though.

"I stopped living according to my core values. I knew what I was doing was wrong but thought only about myself and thought I could get away with whatever I wanted to."

—Tiger Woods, golfer—after his fall from grace

6

Getting Your Client to Go with Their Gut Instinct

Before we start the values process, please bear with me while we take another slight detour because I want to explain how I set the client up to get the best and most accurate results possible.

When I am coaching clients, I am always paying attention to the first response I get to almost any question because that's often the most authentic one.

Let's suppose I ask a client what her biggest goal in life is and then sit back and wait.

The first response I see is that her face lights up for a split second before she shakes her head, returns to normal, and mutters that she doesn't really know.

But I know she does really know.

The instant I asked the question her unconscious mind threw the answer at her, and that was that split-second response of delight and enthusiasm I saw.

Unfortunately, her conscious mind wasn't far behind bringing its often-erroneous version of reality to the proceedings. That reality could be anything from, "that's too hard," to "you're too old," "you're not smart enough," "you haven't got enough money," "people will laugh at you," etc.

That first response took place at a rapid rate (which is why our gut instinct is often known as rapid cognition) and often too quickly for the client to even be aware it happened at all. She was merely left holding the reason or excuse given to her by her conscious mind that was desperate to maintain the status quo and protect her from the danger of daring and failing.

Whether you're conducting The Clarity Method™, or are in any coaching environment, if you see the person you are working with display an emotion or response that almost immediately disappears and is replaced by something entirely different, don't shake it off or ignore it. It's easy to think you were imagining something but you probably weren't. As human beings, we are excellent at reading subtle cues like that. We just choose to ignore them for the most part.

I advise asking something like, "I get a sense that there may be something else. Something that perhaps you feel is unattainable or outside of your reach at the moment. What do you think it could be?"

The question at the end contains a presupposition that there is something you don't know. Asking, "Am I right?" is more likely to elicit a negative response and asking, "What is it?" a reply of, "I don't know." Saying, "What do you think it could it be?" gives the person more latitude. Using the word "could" removes the pressure that they have to come up with a solution or that any solution has to be correct.

The more you give people who you are coaching the space and freedom to let their imagination run wild, the better results you will achieve.

Now you're going to take people through a head-to-head evaluation comparing every value on their list to every other value, and you want them to move through the process as quickly as reasonably possible. You really don't want them taking more than a second or so at each stage, because you want their answers coming from their gut instinct.

If you don't explain this clearly and get the client's buy-in, there is a good possibility they will start to analyze each value comparison to death. Not only will the process take forever but you may well end up with lists of values your clients think they should have, rather than what they do have. You can assure them that you're not chiseling their answers in stone and that it's fine to change the results afterward if they don't feel right.

This is where I will explain (unless it has come up prior to now, in which case I will refer back to our previous conversation) what a gut feeling is, why they are so important, and why I want the client to tap into his or hers right now.

Gut instinct sounds a tad woo-woo and vague but fortunately science has proven that not only does it exist in the form of the aforementioned rapid cognition, but also that it can be foolish to ignore.

Note: On top of what is known about rapid cognition, there is now a strong growing belief that there is a mini-brain residing in the gut that communicates directly with the brain. It has been known for some time that there is something called the brain-gut axis comprised of millions of neurons connecting the brain to the enteric nervous system in the gut.

This is what can cause that literal sinking feeling you can feel in your stomach on hearing bad news. However, the array of neurons in the enteric system is way more complex than is necessary to only deal with digestion, hence suggesting that it has a larger role in thinking than was previously thought to be the case.

One of the best demonstrations of gut instinct was an experiment called the Iowa Gambling Test. The original experiment was conducted by Damasio, Bechara, Tranel, and

Anderson in 1994 and brought into the mainstream by neuroscientist Antonio Damasio.

Participants were wired up so that their unconscious responses such as skin temperature, perspiration, blood pressure, etc. could be scientifically measured. They were then shown four decks of cards on a computer screen and given $2,000 to play with.

The rules of the test were that they would be given 100 turns. Each turn consisted of selecting one of the four decks on the screen. Once a deck was selected, the computer would tell the participant that they either won or lost money, and how much. After each turn, they were free to draw another card from the same deck or move to another deck.

What the participants didn't know was that the decks were rigged. Two packs gave small but regular gains when selected consistently, and if the participant kept choosing those decks, they would make money over the course of the 100 turns. The other two packs, however, gave some large payouts but also large losses. If consistently selected, those decks would result in the participant losing all their money by the end of the experiment.

The results were astounding.

On average, it took the drawing of 80 cards before players could confidently explain why they were drawing from one deck and not another. About 30 cards prior to that, they had started drawing solely from the correct decks, but weren't quite sure why.

A staggering 70 cards before they knew why, they were getting sensory feedback from their body indicating where to take the cards from. In other words, after just 10 cards their unconscious knew where to take the cards from, even if the players showed zero conscious awareness.

Not surprisingly, a common trait among successful gamblers is their possession of a very high level of intrapersonal skills—one of the seven intelligences as discussed in *Frames of Mind*, the groundbreaking book on multiple intelligences by Howard Gardner.

Not only are they highly skilled at reading other people's body language but they are masters at tapping into their unconscious mind. By deciphering what the feelings and emotions they are experiencing mean, they can go with the flow and play on instinct.

If clients know how their unconscious mind works and how they can spot unconscious feelings, they will not just have more success with the process but you have given them a great tool they can use for the rest of their lives. So consider this a bonus section!

Here is how I tend to introduce this part for most clients (like I said earlier, presuming we haven't already had a conversation about gut instincts):

"I'm pretty sure you get strong gut feelings or intuition from time to time. A sense from deep within that a decision you're about to make is either right or wrong.

I'm equally sure that you override that feeling at least occasionally and then wonder why afterward, right? Think of all the times you have said to yourself after you have made a decision, 'I knew I shouldn't have done that,' or, 'I just knew that person wasn't who they said they were.' That was because your unconscious mind was on the case weighing up all the evidence at its disposal and trying to communicate its findings to you, but you weren't listening.

You really shouldn't be tough on yourself, because it's not your fault. It's actually your prefrontal cortex (or conscious mind, if you will), getting involved in something that's quite frankly none of its business.

The rest of your brain is a beautiful and highly efficient thing that has evolved over hundreds of thousands of years and knows a thing or two about life. Your prefrontal cortex—which is responsible for your executive functions such as decision making, planning, and conscious behavior, and which reflects your personality—not so much."

I read a brilliant analogy in David Rock's outstanding book, *Your Brain at Work*, that will give you a clear idea of the difference between your conscious and unconscious mind when it comes to computing power.

If you think of your conscious mind as being the change in your pocket and your unconscious mind as the wealth of the US economy, you get a fairly accurate idea of the imbalance of power between the two parts of your brain.

Your unconscious mind can literally be doing hundreds of things at once. It's beating your heart, maintaining your blood pressure, digesting your food, converting that food into glucose for energy, monitoring every single nerve cell for damage, and it's constantly on the lookout for potential danger.

It's evolved over 3,000,000 years and is a finely tuned machine, whereas your conscious mind gets all stressed and whiny if you ask it to do just two things at once. Thus, whilst you may think you're multitasking, you're really just going back and forth very quickly between tasks.

I could tell you that there is a small fraction of people who, according to Professors David Sanbonmatsu and David Strayer from the University of Utah, can effectively multitask. But I'm not going to because even though the figure is less than 2%, you will presume you are one of the gifted few and think you're safe texting and driving at the same time. You're not; don't do it!

What happens prior to your having a strong gut instinct is your unconscious mind moves into rapid cognition mode. It does a load of nifty lightning-fast calculations, weighs up the odds of success versus failure, and then sends you what it thinks is the appropriate signal.

It then sits back with a big cigar and glass of fine brandy, relaxed in the knowledge it did its job and now it's down to you to use the information wisely.

Unfortunately, even though it has massive computational power, your brain is also a bit like one of those huge old supercomputers from the 1970s. You have to know what the data it spits out actually means because it's not always clear.

A gut feeling really can be a gut feeling, or it can literally be a stomach ache brought on by eating dodgy chili at a hole-in-the-wall Mexican restaurant the previous night. And that's partly the reason so many people don't go with their gut feelings as much as they could or should. It's not that they're not there, it's just that people either don't trust them, rationalize them away, or don't notice them until after the event.

The other reason is that some people struggle to know the difference between a gut feeling and wussing out from a tough decision.

The truth is, you're chattering away to yourself like a demented gibbon 24 hours a day, seven days a week. We all are because it is what we have trained our minds to do.

If you doubt that, close your eyes for a moment and focus all your attention on your breath. Unless you're an experienced meditator, my money says you can't go five seconds without a thought (and thoughts are language) popping into your mind.

That's not a problem, though; it's just what your mind does to get you through the day. And, this side of being in a coma or deep trance, we're all in the same boat when it comes to this.

However, an internal conversation is not the same thing as a gut feeling. The reason is that gut feelings don't usually come in the form of spoken language; they are almost always kinesthetic, or at least start kinesthetically—as feelings—rather than thoughts.

The following internal conversations are almost certainly not gut feelings:

- Don't publish that blog post—It's too controversial and people will criticize you, and you know how much you hate being criticized. Better safe than sorry.

- If you start up your own coaching business, it's bound to fail—because you're a loser and that lemonade stand you started when you were six years old failed, so what makes you think this will be any different?

- We are fine just as we are—we don't need to lose weight, get fit, or quit smoking. After all we have to die someday anyway, so why not enjoy ourselves whilst we're still around?

They are conversations stemming from your conscious mind that's getting all fearful about being dragged out of its comfort zone and is trying to con you into thinking you're about to make a bad decision.

Sometimes I will need to go into more detail because the client may ask me how to spot a gut feeling. If so, then I will explain further. Although I probably won't go into this level of detail regularly purely because of time constraints (I want to get the values finished in one session so I don't lose all momentum and have to pick it up again next time), I do want to give you a sense of how far you can take it if you think it has value. So, here is what I might say to a client:

"My guess is you're already way better at spotting your gut instincts than you give yourself credit for. You may ignore them because of the reasons I just explained—they don't seem to make sense on the surface—but that's not the same thing as not spotting them.

What I want you to do now is think of a handful of occasions in which you had a strong gut feeling that turned out to be correct. Now I want you to look for common denominators:

- Where did the feeling emanate from?

- What type of feeling was it?

- How long did it last?

- Was it constant or did it ebb and flow?

- Was it a slow awareness or did it hit you like a freight train?

The more information you gather at this stage, the better equipped you'll be to spot the next gut instinct you have because they have a strong tendency to replicate one another.

If you can't remember in any detail, that's cool because you get to track your gut feelings from here on in and really get a glimpse into your own psyche and what makes you tick.

Once you have as many details as possible, you're ready to spot your next gut instinct but you really do have to pay attention. When you get that sense that something is either right or wrong, see if it measures up to previous occasions. And if it does, my advice would be to go with it."

Gut instincts can and will be wrong from time to time so don't spend your life responding entirely to gut instincts and ignoring overwhelming contrary evidence.

I once heard a story about three people who were working on a farm in the Midwest. Without warning, a raging grass fire started quite some way from them but was moving in their direction.

Depending on the weather and wind speed, wildfires can move at up to 15 miles per hour which is fast when you consider that the world-record holder for the marathon doesn't hit that speed.

All three instinctively started to run (gut instinct), but one had the presence of mind to realize he couldn't outrun it for more than a short distance. He stopped, took stock, and on spotting a small but steep slope started to remove all the brush around him for a few feet so there was no combustible material.

He then curled up in a ball and waited. Although receiving some nasty burns, he was the only one of the three to survive, and that was thanks to him questioning his initial urge to run and engaging in critical thinking. However, I think we can agree that was an extreme example.

Let's suppose you are about to walk into a Miami bank in July and in front of you are four men carrying duffel bags and wearing ski masks. It's doubtful you will have had time to register that information at a conscious level before you have already started to turn around, thinking, "You know what, I reckon I'll get lunch first."

That is because a pair of almond-sized and almond-shaped nuclei called the amygdala (part of the limbic system, buried deep within the medial temporal lobes of your brain) have kicked into action, alerting you of danger without the need to bother you at a conscious level first.

Your amygdala is screaming, "Danger, danger, Will Robinson!" before you have even had time to think about taking your shades off. (Unless, of course, your name is Jenny, in which case it will probably use that name. And apologies for the lame "Lost in Space" reference and showing my age.)

Think about all those times you have sensed danger when, on reflection, you didn't know why. Now, thank your amygdala because it may have literally saved your life on occasion.

I have a confession to make. I used to ignore my gut instinct in my early days of coaching. Four or five times I had a gut instinct that a client wasn't a good fit for me. Yet I took him or her on after going through a lot of self-justification and convincing myself that I could make it work.

On every single occasion, I regretted burying my gut instinct and working with that person, as I had created a lose-lose scenario.

Whether you are a coach, a manager, or a businessperson, there will always be times when you should say no to either a potential client, customer, or employee even though it may cost you money in the short term.

Interestingly enough, as I was writing this section, I received a phone call from a guy who wanted to joint venture with me. He wanted to know if I'd run an ad for his products in my newsletter or on my blog. It would have been an easy $100, but I said no. And the reason was that it really didn't feel right. I didn't feel like I should be supporting a product for financial gain when I wasn't sure it would benefit my readers or clients.

Bye-bye $100. Hello integrity and peace of mind.

Important Note: There is a very small part of the population who don't get gut responses. For the most part, this is irrelevant to you as it's doubtful you will be working with people who have conditions such as autism, which can dampen gut instincts. However, people who were emotionally or physically abused in childhood may similarly struggle. Oh, and by the way, just in case you were wondering, science pretty much agrees that women do tend to have better instincts. Sorry, guys!

"Everyone needs a coach."

—*Bill Gates, co-founder of Microsoft*

7

Time to Do the Work: Matrixing Your Client's Values

The values matrixing process I am about to take you through is the one that I nearly always use with clients. However, if after you have watched the video and read the alternative approach I detail in the next chapter, you prefer that method, then be my guest.

However, I don't want you to default to Option 2 just because it seems easier and the spreadsheet for Option 1 looks a tad complicated at first glance. It only looks that way, and if you're smart enough to tie your shoelaces and talk at the same time, then you will soon get the hang of it.

It may be that you even decide to mix and match depending on the person and which approach you think they will be more receptive to. There have been occasions when a client has gotten so wrapped up in analyzing that I have switched to the second method to see if that helps unblock them. By and large, the more academic and left-brained the client, the more apt I am to switch to the process I was first taught in my life coach training.

As I say, the form can look a bit daunting, but it's incredibly simple to use once you get the hang of it. Rather than explain it in writing for you, I have made a lovely video for you to watch in case you still have any lingering doubts. And you can find the forms I used in the video in the addendum at the end of the book or go to www.claritymethod.com/bookstuff

Hang on a minute, though. Before you watch the video, I want to explain how you can use the matrix form to order pretty much anything you want quickly and accurately.

I once worked with a client who had six separate projects on the go at the same time. He just couldn't make his mind up which was best for him, and he was getting bogged down in the minutiae of each project rather than moving forward with a route to market and making money.

Your brain loves having choices. In fact, a lack of choice is, along with the removal of autonomy, the cause of all stress in people's lives. [2] However, even though your brain likes some choice, it's very persnickety and hates too much choice almost as much as too little.

If you have ever got overwhelmed by a huge menu in a restaurant like The Cheesecake Factory, the choice of 101 different shades of off-white when you are looking to paint your front room, or which book to buy when browsing a good old-fashioned bookstore, you will have experienced what that feels like. It can literally cause people to be mentally paralyzed and shut down, unable to make any decision at all.

It feels so bad because as we've already touched on, your conscious mind cannot process more than about three or four pieces of information at once, and after that it starts having to delete things. [3]

Thinking about six projects at once is literally impossible for any human being; the prefrontal cortex will go on strike and refuse to play ball.

Even though your unconscious is chilled to the bone at seeing all that choice, the chances of it muscling its way past your stressed-out conscious mind with a clear enough message for you to understand what it's saying is slim to none.

There was a famous experiment conducted by Professor Sheena Iyengar from Columbia University involving Wilkin & Sons jam company.

Her team set up stalls in a California food market offering free jam samples with a $1 off coupon to people who participated.

They would offer six jams for a while and then swap that and offer 24 types of jams. Fifty percent more people stopped at the stall with the larger selection but something very weird happened.

Of the people who had 24 jams to choose from, only 3% went on to use the coupon and buy. Whereas 30% of people who were presented with less choice decided to make a purchase. The first group—overwhelmed with choice—simply decided not to decide. Sometimes too much choice is not a good thing.

The matrix form allows you to do comparisons one at a time. Your brain loves binary information and can deal with it in stride.

Incidentally, this is why so many people have such dogmatic opinions when it comes to things like politics. Your brain much prefers to think that its choice of a political party is the right choice. As such, it wants to think that every decision it makes is correct.

Of course, some people can and do invoke critical thinking, but unless you have trained it to do so, your brain isn't that keen on entertaining grey areas.

With the client who had the six live projects, we simply entered in a word for each project, and then ran through the form with me asking him to compare each project against the other.

By the end, it was clear which one was the one he really wanted to do, even if prior to then he thought he had no idea. He was delighted and I looked like a genius. Cool eh?

For the purpose of the demonstration, I am going to take eight things off my bucket list and compare them head-to-head to show you how simple it is. I'm actually quite excited as I type this, because I genuinely have no idea which order they will fall in.

So, rather than talking about this now, go to www.claritymethod.com/bookstuff to watch the video. Whilst you are there you can see the matrix form (just a spreadsheet, there will be no swallowing of either blue or red tablets unless you have a headache and are planning on taking an Excedrin). You are going to need two of these spreadsheets shortly, so download them now.

After you watch the video, we can arrange your hierarchy of values.

Okay, so you have watched the video and downloaded two copies of the matrix, haven't you? I'm trusting you; and if you haven't, I will feel compelled to slaughter the cutest baby bunny rabbit I can find and drink its sweet warm blood as punishment. So, don't say I haven't warned you when Big Ears gets it.

Now list your values in the 8 boxes down the left-hand side on one, and your anti-values on the other. Remember, I want you to move through the process quickly and tap into your unconscious mind in the same way you will want to do with people whom you are helping.

The next page shows an example of what the sheet may look like prior to your starting. And we are in complete agreement that for this part of the process, analyzing is bad, right? Excellent! Well, off you go to order your values. I'll feed the rabbit and we will both be waiting for you on your return.

Footnotes:

2. If you want to simplify this even more, you can do so by just saying that a lack of control is the root of all stress.

3. Prior to the advent of functional MRI (fMRI) machines, common wisdom was that the mind could process between five and nine pieces of information. We now know this to be completely out of our capabilities and that even pigeons can multitask better than we can.

THE CLARITY METHOD

No	Value	Ranking							Score
1	Integrity	1	1	1	1	1	1	1	
		2	3	4	5	6	7	8	
2	Freedom	2	2	2	2	2	2		
		3	4	5	6	7	8		
3	Humor	3	3	3	3	3			
		4	5	6	7	8			
4	Respect	4	4	4	4				
		5	6	7	8				
5	Humility	5	5	5					
		6	7	8					
6	Peace	6	6						
		7	8						
7	Canaraderie	7							
		8							
8	Authenticity								

"Happiness is that state of consciousness which proceeds from the achievement of one's values.."

—Ayn Rand

8

How to Determine a Client's Hierarchy of Values: An Alternative Method

The method I have just described is actually not how I was trained to do a value elicitation. Not only didn't my original training incorporate anti-values (that was something I adopted later after stumbling across them during some NLP training and realizing they were crucial to completing the process), it also didn't call for showing sample values to clients.

It was a very simple process that involved asking the client the following question: "What is important to you in your life?"

Sometimes the response would throw up an obvious value such as Love, Peace, or Freedom. However, more often than not the answer would be more convoluted, like being able to have plenty of time off, or earning lots of money, and would require the follow up question, "What does X (where X is the response) give you?"

And that question would be asked again and again until a value was reached. You then ask again to ensure that there isn't more than one value attached to the answer—at which point you would revert to the original question and start the process again.

Here is an example:

Coach: "What is important to you in your life?"

Client: "Having more money."

Coach: "What does having more money give you?"

Client: "I can go on more vacations and take more time off."

Coach: "What does having more vacations and taking time off give you?"

Client: "I can spend more time with my family."

At this point we have our first value, that of Family, and we can start the process again.

Coach: "What else does more money give you?"

Clients: "Security, I guess."

Coach: "What does security give you?"

Client: "I'm not really sure, I just would feel more secure, more relaxed."

Sometimes a value pops up immediately as in this case. However, even when that is the case still ask again to make sure there's nothing else in there.

Coach: "What else does money give you?"

Client: "I can buy a bigger house."

Coach: "What does having a bigger house give you?"

Client: "I'm not really sure."

Coach: "If you were sure, what would having a bigger house give you?" [4]

Client: "I'd look like I've made it, that I have succeeded."

Coach: "What does success give you?"

Client: "I don't know. It just feels good."

At some stage, the client will not be able to tell you anything else that money gives them so you start the process again from the beginning with "'What else is important to you in your life?"

When you get words and expressions like *success* and *made it*, you're nearly always dealing with the value of Status. Whereas it's nice to think we are not motivated by status, nothing could be further from the truth—your brain absolutely loves it.

How do you feel if you're having a petty argument with a friend and you suddenly realize half-way through that you're wrong? What about being dumped by a partner? And how do you feel when you get fired, demoted, or turned down for a job?

Depending on your personality, the answer to those questions will be on a line from mildly disappointed to devastated. That feeling may only be fleeting or it may go on for some time, and the reason is largely because you have had a loss of status.

Winning an argument, getting a 'yes' when asking for a date or getting a job creates a dopamine rush that makes us feel great. But when the opposite happens, we get a dopamine crash and feel miserable.

It's probably wise not to be bothered about status, but it's a big ask. It's a bit like saying don't be bothered by fear. Is it possible? Possibly with a few decades of solid meditation, but a desire for status is hardwired into us and as such we have to acknowledge it as coaches.

There is one huge upside to this approach, and that is that the process retains complete integrity. By that I mean you cannot give your client an easy out by showing a list and giving her the opportunity to choose eight off that list. (As we have discussed, some people will take that route if offered it.)

You also remove the risk of priming the client with values that they may not actually have but think they should have when they look at the sample sheet.

Note: Just in case you're not familiar with priming, it is a term used in social psychology and refers to our tendency to be influenced by things outside of our conscious awareness. In one famous experiment conducted in 1996 at New York University by social psychologist John Bargh, students were given a test that involved unscrambling words into groups as quickly as they could.

Like so many such experiments, that wasn't the real purpose of the exercise. Unbeknownst to the students, half of them were exposed to a lot of words that we commonly associate with the elderly, like retirement, tired, old, etc., whereas the other half (the control group) was not.

When they finished the test, the students were secretly timed to see how long it took them to walk a short corridor after handing in their paper. The students who had been exposed to the words signifying old age took, on average, a full second longer (eight seconds as opposed to seven) to cover the distance.

There have been mixed results with people trying to replicate this research but it's still a great way to understand the impact priming can have.

On the other hand, there are a number of downsides to doing things this way, which are:

1. It can be an incredibly time-consuming and laborious process.

2. The client can lose interest or get frustrated, especially if they are struggling to answer.

3. The client may simply forget about something that is really important to them.

4. You don't get the opportunity to have the client thinking about values prior to the session.

Obviously, I prefer the method I use but I can see benefits of both, and I'd advise you to use whichever one feels right to you and your client. Having both methods at your disposal means you can mix and match depending on your client. Certainly knowing the method I just outlined is very cool if you simply want to do an impromptu values session with somebody you have not had chance to prepare with.

Once you have your two lists, you're going to take a closer look for both internal and external value conflicts, so that when you understand why they are so important later in the book you can give them a damn good thrashing ... probably.

———————

Footnote:

4. In the example above, you would think that if a client has already told me that they don't know the answer to a question, then asking them, "But what if you did know?" would elicit a look of incredulity and a response of, "What are you talking about? I just told you I don't know?" But that is seldom the case and it will frequently result in an answer you can work with. I will even take it a stage further if I get another "I don't know." I'll laugh and then say something like, "Okay I get that, but we're just messing around here. Have a guess. What would the answer be?" Don't be afraid to give your clients permission to dream because you'll be amazed at what you can uncover.

"Your values create your internal compass that can navigate how you make decisions in your life. If you compromise your core values, you go nowhere."

—*Roy T. Bennett, author of The Light in The Heart*

9

These Are the Values—What Do I Do With Them?

Before we get into what you do with your values and how you will use your clients' values to help them, let's do a bit of due diligence to make sure what you have is as accurate as we can get it.

The first question is, are you surprised by your list?

Don't worry if you're not; that's not a problem at all. It's just that I frequently hear comments such as, "Wow, I never expected X value to be so high," or "I really thought Y value was more important to me than that."

As I said, the process you used to order them is very basic, but like a lot of basic things it is very effective, and the list you now have is way more likely to be correct than doing it analytically.

Having said that, the chances that you've nailed your top eight values in exactly the right order are, if not zero, then close to it because values are always somewhat contextual or situational.

By this, I mean values that may be important to you when working with clients may not be relevant when you are out with friends or spending family time. That's important to understand and to help your clients understand.

Imagine somebody with a number-one value of Fun who happens to be an undertaker (and trust me, clients like this will exist). I'm sure he can have fun when working because any job can be fun if you love your work. However, when he is meeting the deceased's family, telling jokes or turning up dressed as a clown and driving a tiny car may be less than appropriate.

And that, while it may be an extreme example, is what I mean about contextual or situational. We cannot be in alignment with all of our values all of the time, and some will ebb and flow in importance depending on the circumstances and situation.

Having said this, your values should be very close to being spot on and certainly close enough to give you a better understanding of yourself and what's most important to you.

As you look at the list, does it feel right?

Do those values sum up you as a person?

Do they make you smile, even?

Do you want to pump the air and say, "Yeah baby, I'm ready to take on the world—to the Batmobile—let's go! Damn, I don't have a Batmobile. Oh well—to the Toyota Corolla—let's go!"

Hopefully you answered 'yes' to all those questions. If you didn't and actually said 'no' to all of them, I want you to turn right around and go back to the beginning without passing Go or collecting $200.

Similarly, when you do the process with another person and he or she looks or sounds flat or less than engaged, dig a little deeper. This rarely happens, but don't be afraid to challenge a client or the person you are coaching if it does.

If you've built a good level of rapport, you really can—and quite frequently should—challenge your clients. And if you think you can't, then you're either not in rapport—which is a major problem—or you haven't set up their expectations at the beginning of the call or when starting the coaching process. You must feel safe in challenging the people you are coaching. And similarly, you should feel comfortable being challenged yourself. No excuses.

On the other hand, if you get a sense that the values you have are there or thereabouts but that there may be something missing, that's cool. Worry not.

If you come up with a word that you suspect should be on your list but you're not really sure, simply compare it with whatever is at number eight on your list and ask yourself if it's more important to you. If it is more important, do the same thing with number seven and keep working your way through your values until you find its slot. Then, *hey, presto!*, you have a top nine list rather than a top eight list. And by the way, this is often what I do when clients send me more than eight values. Rather than expand the form, I slot them in at the end.

If you're still not convinced that they're totally right or think there may be a value or two missing but can't quite put your finger on which ones, I'd encourage you to do the following. And yes, you can suggest this approach to somebody you are coaching and get them to do the same. It will of course lengthen the process but that is preferable than trying to rush it and getting it wrong.

Print your values list and put it in a drawer and forget about it for at least a day or so, maybe even a few days if you can do so. The last thing I want you doing at this stage is try to analyze it to death and stress yourself because you think you're not doing it right or you have some wrong values.

Go and enjoy an aperitif of your choice with my blessing and congratulate yourself on a job well done and chill out. This is long-term and dynamic work we're doing here, and unless you're about to propose marriage to somebody you met last night or single-handedly invade a small sovereign territory, another day or so probably won't make that much difference.

Over the next day (or however long you choose to leave it), pay attention to and WRITE DOWN any words or phrases that jump into your mind that are value-related.

As you know by now, your unconscious mind is absolutely brilliant at providing you answers to questions when you least expect them. Unfortunately, though, most people aren't paying attention to their hard-working brain, or they simply forget and the unconscious storms off in a huff because it feels ignored.

That's why you get some of your best ideas when your conscious mind is tied up doing other things. As an example, if I can't think of anything to write about for a blog post, I know without a shadow of a doubt that if I avoid Words With Friends and instead stick some music on my iPhone and go to the gym, an idea will come to me in no time at all. Seriously, it never fails.

Similarly, I know that I get some of my more creative ideas when I'm in the half-asleep-and-half-awake stage when my unconscious mind comes to the fore and can weave its magic (or stupidity, as my wife tends to think of it).

Einstein got the idea for special relativity (and probably his bagel company, too) whilst laid up in bed sick with the flu. And Dr. James Watson took it a stage further by figuring out the structure of the DNA double helix whilst dreaming about a snake eating itself! If it's good enough for those giants of science, then it's good enough for you and me.

The next day, go back to your list and give it a cursory glance to see how it feels to you. And yes, I do mean how it *feels*. I don't care how it looks, because if I haven't hammered the message home enough already, this is your unconscious mind we're dealing with. It loves to work with feelings and could care less about everything else for the most part.

Again, if it doesn't feel quite right, that's cool. Worry not. Simply do the exercise again and see if you get the same results.

Note: Don't worry if you have values that score the same. If there are two that are tied, you can split them by doing a head-to-head. If I get a client with three or even four that are the same, I'm most likely to leave them in place because it just means they are really close together. Every now and then, I may want to split them up, such as when a client is struggling with deciding and has competing values, but it's very rare. And there is always the option of doing the process again from scratch and then working out almost an average of the results.

You may think that you're wasting a client's time doing this twice, but you run the risk of wasting much more time and sending them off in the wrong direction if you get it wrong.

I realize that doing the exercise yourself affords you the luxury of breaking off for a day or two. Obviously, this isn't always possible with clients but don't be afraid to end the process and give your client the same instructions I just gave you so you can pick it up next time. I know that's not ideal and it won't happen very often but we want the process to work and need to be flexible.

In the next two chapters, I'm going to explain what external and internal value conflicts are. We are really getting into the meat of the what The Clarity Method™ means and can deliver now, and I encourage you to make sure the people you are coaching fully understand this part—because if they don't, the whole process loses a lot of its value and impact.

"A core value is something you're willing to get punished for."

—Patrick Lencioni, author of The Five Dysfunctions of a Team

10

What Is an External Value Conflict?

External value conflicts are everywhere you look, from the individual level all the way up to a societal level, with all stops in between. The earlier example of the social media furor that preceded the 2008 and subsequent general elections was a classic example of external value conflicts on a rampage. And that has been exacerbated tenfold with the arrival of Donald Trump at the White House.

The women who marched on Washington D.C. after his election win did so because they felt like they were having their values trampled on by the incoming administration.

Similarly, the Native Americans (and their supporters) at Standing Rock who were protesting the Dakota Access Pipeline were doing so not just for the sake of preserving their land but because of what that land stood for.

If you have a dislike for a certain person or feel uncomfortable in his or her presence, it will, presuming they haven't got terrible body odor, almost certainly be value-based. Maybe she is racist and you value tolerance, or she is aggressive and you value peace. Or maybe even that you abhor conflict and she is always getting into petty arguments and squabbles.

When I was in sales, I once took a client out for lunch to discuss a potential deal. I didn't know him very well, but we'd always got on well on the phone as we both had a strong interest in football (known in the States as soccer).

We went to a local gastro pub and sat down to peruse the menu. After a few minutes, I took our orders back to the bar, then returned to the table where we chatted pleasantly as we waited for our food. I wasn't really ready for what happened next after the server dropped off the meal.

In fairness, the food wasn't really deserving of the word 'gastro' unless it meant you were likely to contract gastroenteritis by eating it, but it was no big deal. This was the late '80s, and we were used to terrible pub food in those days in England (it's got a lot better—honest!).

I have zero problem with complaining about poor service, poor food, or poor anything if it deserves it. As somebody who has owned a retail outlet and also managed a restaurant, it's important to know if there are issues. You cannot rectify problems you're unaware of, so there's nothing wrong in people complaining respectfully as it can actually help you improve your products or services.

But there's an art to complaining and it doesn't involve swearing loudly and aggressively at the person behind the bar (who didn't cook the meal and wasn't even the owner), refusing to pay (a little stupid as I had already paid when I ordered the food), and then storming out leaving your guest apologizing profusely—all of which my very rude client did.

I value tolerance very highly. Does that mean I'm always tolerant? No, of course not; it can be tricky at times. But probably the most irritating part of this whole escapade was the complete contempt my client had shown to the barman who had merely taken the order.

Any of those reasons I just mentioned can be enough (if the value is important to you) to cause, if not dislike, at least a desire to avoid the company of the other person. From then on in, I did my best to eschew my client and wasn't sad when a few weeks later I called to speak with him only to find out he'd left the business.

Such individual external value conflicts are definitely something I'm looking out for with clients. However, I'm sometimes more interested in value conflicts turning up in the working environment, as these can be a massive roadblock to happiness and fulfillment and something you want to be constantly on the lookout for with people who you are taking through The Clarity Method™.

I spent my last 10 years in sales not exactly job-hopping, but certainly not settling in one place. It seems that wherever I worked I felt uncomfortable with some of the things I was asked to do.

At that time, I knew nothing about value conflicts and just presumed that compromise was the name of the game when it came to sales. Sure, I could have taken a stand and resigned from my job after the gastropub debacle, but I'm not sure what it would have achieved other than my having to find another job

I liked to think I was an ethical salesperson and was constantly looking to create win-win situations for my customers. I always thought that the biggest buzz in sales wasn't getting an order from a new client but rather getting a repeat order. People tend not to buy twice from somebody who mis-sold them in the first place, so when people re-order you know they trust you and that you did your job properly.

To create win-win situations meant it was important I understand their specific business needs, their pain points and their goals, and then find a product or service to meet their needs, ease their pain, and help them move toward their goals.

Most sales organizations have more than one product or service to sell, and quite often there can be dozens or even hundreds. Therefore, if you are working for a half-decent and reputable company, it's not usually difficult to find a product or service that works for any one customer and creates that win-win scenario.

Until, that is, you get hit by something called a 'product drive.' A product drive is when the word comes down (usually) from senior management that the business is behind quota or target on a certain product or service and thus a heavy push for sales is required, sometimes to the exclusion of all other products or services.

I guess it's not much different than a waiter in a restaurant suggesting the mushroom soup is delicious because he knows the chef got hammered on cooking sherry last night and made fifty gallons of the stuff that will get wasted if they don't steer customers toward it.

Selling somebody a bowl of soup they weren't that bothered about is a tad manipulative, I guess, but in the grand scheme of things it's probably not a big deal. Especially as the customer can see the rest of the menu and order something else should they so wish. A product drive, though, can be akin to hiding the menu entirely.

Selling somebody a service that is going to cost in excess of $100K when you know you have a $50K version that will do the job equally well is another matter altogether. It's dishonest, unethical, and lacks any integrity whatsoever. Sadly, it also goes on a lot more than you would care to realize in the world of big-ticket sales.

In one of the last sales jobs I took, I specifically asked the people interviewing me if they ever imposed product drives and I was assured they didn't. I took the job and within six months was subjected to a huge product drive. I could have wept.

Needless to say, I didn't last long in that job because I had a couple of massive value conflicts staring me in the face. Not only was I being asked to do something I thought was unethical, but I had also been lied to at the interview stage. I decided that I didn't want to work for a company who would tell me exactly what I wanted to hear irrespective of the consequences.

The problem with company values is that they are seldom visible from the outside. Or if they are, it can be difficult to be sure if they are true or not. If you had checked the Enron company website prior to applying to work for them before their bankruptcy in 2001, you would have probably been impressed to see that the company's values were:

- Respect

- Integrity

- Communication

- Excellence

I mean, come on. I know core values are subjective, but who wouldn't be enamored by such values and who wouldn't want to work for such a great company, even if they aren't necessarily the values you would choose? Of course, we now know the values their senior management team wanted people to see were not the values that their actions and deeds were aligned with.

Twenty thousand people lost their jobs at Enron because senior management had built a company based on lies, corruption, and highly creative accounting practices rather than Respect, Integrity, Communication, and Excellence.

And therein lies the danger. Trying to figure out how a company really operates at the level of values in an hour-long interview is close to impossible. In fact, unless you know somebody on the inside who will be honest with you, you are often rolling the dice.

No company is going to tell you they don't give a damn about their clients as long as the bottom line looks rosy. Or that they are perfectly happy to drive their employees toward stress-induced illness just to hit quotas and keep stockholders happy.

I'll give you a great example. When I went to work for the behemoth that was Yell (formerly called Yellow Pages), they had a reputation in the sales industry that was second to none. Their initial and ongoing training was outstanding, the pay was excellent for a non-IT company, and the overall package with company car and very generous expenses were quite something to drool over. Not only that, but they had won the award for the best European company—the European Quality Award—just prior to my joining.

Once a business had won the European Quality Award, they were precluded from entering again for five years. Yell wanted to be the first company in the history of the award to win it twice. How badly did they want to win it?

Badly enough to cheat, that's how badly.

The award application forms filled in by employees were supposed to be confidential so that everybody could answer honestly about what it was like to work for Yell. Sadly, it was made abundantly clear that our managers were going to be checking our forms before they were accepted. We all knew that giving answers that cast Yell in a bad light would lead to repercussions.

I could go on and on about some of the things that went on in the three years I worked for Yell, and many would astound you. Let's just leave it by my saying the company had obviously had an integrity bypass operation and had little regard for anything other than profit and market share.

There are exceptions to organizations like Yell, of course. Companies like Virgin, Zappos, Nordstrom, Google, and Apple have made a name for themselves by treating employees and customers alike with—for the large part—respect and integrity.

At the time of writing, Zappos offers new employees $2,000 to leave the business. Yes, that's right. They hire them and then offer to pay them to leave. Why? Because they don't want employees who haven't entirely bought into their culture and who are merely focused on the money. Even after their sale to Amazon for almost one billion dollars, Amazon senior management were savvy enough not to interfere with this approach.

> *As Sir Richard Branson once said, "Clients do not come first. Employees come first. If you take care of your employees, they will take care of your clients."*

And Branson wasn't all talk; he delivered. When I had a record store back in the early '90s, we had about 15 record company representatives visit us each week. Fourteen of the 15 wanted to work for Virgin. The other already did.

One year around then, Branson sent a handwritten Christmas card to every employee in the Virgin Group. Now that's what I call living your values.

The sad thing is, some older businesses don't realize that operating with integrity—valuing employees' downtime (in fact insisting on it), constantly seeking employees' honest feedback on how to make things better (and acting on it), and helping them realize they are important to the well-being of the company, and that their work is meaningful—helps the bottom line.

Happy employees are productive employees.

In his book, *Pre-suasion*, influence expert Robert Cialdini discusses the importance of a company discovering and then adopting its core values, and the incredibly negative impact it can have on the bottom line when they don't follow through with this.

I have had jobs where even though we weren't necessarily told to go out and rip off our customers, it was tacitly accepted and in no way discouraged. Unless, that is, it was so flagrant that the customer backlash and potentially negative publicity would mean it wasn't financially worthwhile.

However, Cialdini explains that when companies turn a blind eye to their employees' transgressions to benefit the short-term profitability of the business, there is an unwanted price to pay on their long-term success.

When you create an atmosphere of dishonesty and winning at all costs, you cannot contain that in any one area. Salespeople who are rewarded when they close deals by utilizing dubious tactics are then exponentially more likely to use those, or similar, tactics to their employer's disadvantage.

In other words, they are far more likely to falsify expense reports, undermine peers and take credit for their work, take sick days when they aren't ill, and ultimately leave for another job that pays more. If you live by the sword, you die by the sword.

The corporate sector in the US loses tens of billions of dollars per year because of the above, and a good proportion of it is avoidable if they utilize the power of core values.

Unfortunately, most companies are too short-sighted and set in their ways to make such a fundamental and necessary shift. As such, most people don't get the opportunity to interview for progressive, value-centered businesses and accordingly, they are usually very much in the dark prior to starting employment.

The best advice we can offer our clients if they find themselves in such a situation (if you even feel comfortable offering advice, as some coaches prefer never to do so) is to try and get them to speak to employees and ask them for as much information as possible that will reveal the values of the organization. Even better still, they could ask ex-employees who left of their own volition. In other words, they haven't been fired and now hold a grudge. I know that may seem like overkill but we spend half our waking life at work, so I happen to think it's worth it whenever possible.

If that isn't possible, and I understand it often won't be, then refer them back to the conversation about gut instincts and tell them to listen carefully to their intuition during the interview process.

In retrospect, I had enough warning signs at the interview I mentioned above to know I was making a monumental mistake; I just foolishly chose to ignore them.

Similarly, when interviewing for my very last sales job, I had already concluded this company wasn't right for me when they offered me a £15K 'golden hello.' Suddenly the chance of earning £15,000 just by signing on helped me bury my gut instinct that was screaming, "Step away from the contract and put the pen down, Brownson!"

I literally stopped at a car dealership on the way home from the interview and ordered a brand new BMW. Even though my wife was a tad concerned when I got home and told her what had happened, I was too busy focusing on the shiny new Beemer I was going to pick up the following day.

Three months later, the process of human adaptation in which we get used to our surroundings and environment had kicked in with full force. The car had lost its luster and I was in a job I despised, not knowing how it had all come to pass.

CASE STUDY - MEET ANDY

Andy came to me because he wanted to change careers but didn't know what he wanted to do. He was in his early forties and had worked in IT as a systems analyst for most of his working life.

For the most part, Andy enjoyed what he did. He was well paid but felt that it was time for a change because it didn't feel right anymore.

It would be easy to take a client like that at face value and start to help build a plan for a new career, but it would also be negligent. As I said earlier, people don't always know what they want because they are so wrapped up in their own lives, and that's why we can help. Everybody, including me, has blind spots and it's a coach's or manager's job to gently shine a light on them.

Doing a value elicitation with a client or colleague who is unhappy in their work can be incredibly revealing. It nearly always throws up numerous value conflicts that demonstrate why the client is feeling that way. Indeed, if you find conflicts with somebody you are managing, you now have a fantastic opportunity to do something about it before you potentially lose a staff member.

However, in this instance with Andy, that didn't happen, and it didn't throw up any obvious conflicts with his job. In fact, just the opposite because it looked to me like the guy was in the perfect role for him. I was totally confused.

We chatted about things for a while and, to be honest, I was struggling to understand why he was unhappy at work. It simply made no sense to me. Until, that is, I asked him about his colleagues and then all was explained.

He didn't have a value conflict with his job or with the company he worked for, but he had a HUGE one with his manager, which he'd neglected to mention. Or if I'm taking responsibility, I had neglected to ask him about.

Andy was a pretty laid-back guy with long hair, tattoos, and a beard. In fact, it wouldn't be unfair to say he looked very much like he had been transported to my office directly from Woodstock.

His manager, on the other hand, was ex-military, and (it would seem) not the most tolerant or easy-going of people. The relaxed atmosphere that Andy had worked in prior to the new manager arriving had been replaced by a much more formal approach and it was stifling to him.

So, his external value conflict wasn't with his role or the company—it was with his boss. The Clarity Method™ had clearly shown that Andy valued tolerance, freedom, and creativity, and his boss, not so much. Unfortunately, Andy had worked in the same job for 15 years and just (incorrectly) presumed that he was burned out or bored by it.

We did a very simple exercise in which I took him on a guided visualization. Visualization is a very under-rated and misunderstood process with many coaches. First, visualization is a misnomer because we utilize as many senses as possible for maximum effect.

Second, when we visualize properly, we engage the areas of the brain as if the event were actually happening. In other words, we fool the brain into believing that what's happening in our imagination is real.

Actors visualize, athletes frequently visualize, public speakers visualize, musicians visualize, and so do many super successful people.

Probably the greatest golfer of all time, Jack Nicklaus didn't just visualize every shot, he visualized every practice shot. Ed Moses, the greatest 400-meter hurdler of all time who was unbeaten for a decade, visualized every stride prior to a race. And Arnold Schwarzenegger used visualization before every event when he was the greatest bodybuilder in the world.

And third, this isn't some woo-woo Law of Attraction thing. Science has proven beyond any doubt that visualization trains the brain to deal with future events. When we visualize, we start to create new neural pathways so that when it comes to undertaking the event in real time, the brain is already prepared.

I wasn't trying to get Andy to form new neural pathways; that takes a bit longer than a sixty-second visualization! But I did want to see what his reaction would be when imagining an ideal scenario.

The exercise involved him arriving at work to find his current boss had resigned and a new manager with a similar outlook to Andy's had taken his place. I asked him to see what he'd see, hear what he'd hear, and allow all the feeling and emotions to arise as they would.

The shift in him was quite remarkable. He was literally smiling, and his entire body language shifted for the better. It was obvious he still liked his work, just not the oppressive atmosphere that he had to conduct it in.

If we'd not used The Clarity Method™ and I'd taken him at his word, he would almost certainly have changed jobs and probably careers when there was really no point. What actually happened was that he decided to look for a new job in the same line of work. If a great one came up, he would interview for it. Early in the job-hunting process, his manager left, and things took a turn for the better. Andy applied for and got his manager's old job. It doesn't always pan out that well, but it can. Such is the power of The Clarity Method™.

Note: Another bonus of working out your values if you're a coach, manager, or an entrepreneur is that it helps you define your ideal client or employee. Not that I'm saying you cannot work with clients or hire people who have different values than you; of course you can, and it's part of your job as a coach and leader to do so. However, there are few things worse in business than having clients or employees who breach your core values.

They will make your life misery and drain you, no matter how much cash they throw in your direction. I once worked with a client whose business was going under. He took great pleasure in showing me a spreadsheet detailing how he extracted $18,000 out of his business the previous month whilst not paying his struggling employees a dime.

We parted company shortly after that, even though at the time I was in my first year or two and struggling to make ends meet. Sometimes you simply cannot square the circle.

"Open your arms to change, but don't let go of your values."

—His Holiness, The Dalai Lama

11

What Is an Internal Value Conflict?

Many people carry internal value conflicts around with them for years (even decades!) and never realize what's going on. They just know something isn't quite right, or worse still, presume this is just how life is but carry on regardless and hope things will get better. If you're a coach or manager, you will start to notice that internal value conflicts can often be the reason people have hired you in the first place in the former example, or why they may appear unhappy at work with the latter.

I have pointed out conflicts to clients that you would have thought would have been obvious to a myopic bat wearing sunglasses. And in no way, shape, or form is that a criticism of any of my clients. It's very much a woods-for-the-trees scenario. It is incredibly difficult to see this stuff when you are right up against it. And I know that from personal experience, because I had my own internal value conflicts for years before I got into coaching, as I have already discussed.

The product drive example I mentioned in Chapter 10 actually threw up external and internal value conflicts. The external conflict was between me and the business I worked for, but the internal one was when I occasionally yielded to pressure against my better judgment. It's a horrible feeling when that happens.

95

All internal value conflicts are not the same, however, and it's important that you don't slip into thinking a client hasn't got any because you have missed one type. So here are three different types of internal conflict:

Type 1: When a client has a value but doesn't practice it (i.e., not in alignment).

Type 2: When a client has values on the opposite side of the equation that cancel one another out.

Type 3: When a client has values on the same side that cancel each other out.

Rather than just explaining what these are, let me give you three examples.

MEET GEOFF—TYPE 1

Geoff had Leadership and Integrity as his top two core values. He hired me because he wasn't maximizing his IT business. He was spending too long each day procrastinating and wasting time on the internet.

He felt demotivated, deflated, and probably discombobulated (I've always wanted to use that word!), and was giving himself a hard time.

After we had walked through The Clarity Method™, I asked him one simple question:

"Do you think you are demonstrating leadership and integrity to your employees, and, if not, do you think you are demonstrating those qualities to yourself?"

That was an *aha!* moment for him because he'd never thought of it like that. I never cease to be amazed at the power of a seemingly simple values-related question like this.

We then implemented a very easy process of him printing out his top three values and sticking them onto his computer screen to remind him why he was really there. And to make sure he didn't become blind to the list, he even programmed his phone to remind him at varying times in the week.

That's about as uncomplicated as it gets, and you will get a lot of quick wins like that because often it's simply a matter of getting the client to focus on what you can already see.

When you work with somebody who feels stuck, has a sense that something feels wrong, or is unhappy with themself and doesn't know why, then that's a good indication that The Clarity Method™ will supply you some answers.

MEET DONNA—TYPE 2

Donna probably handed me the greatest example I have ever seen of a Type 2 internal value conflict—and it was completely paralyzing her. She was in her thirties and married to a man who was more than twenty years her senior. The relationship was cordial and there was no animosity, but on the other hand they hadn't shared a bedroom, or anything else other than passing conversations, in years.

She had decided almost two years earlier that she wanted out of the marriage but simply couldn't pull the trigger on telling her husband, even though she knew it was for the best. They didn't have kids (and she desperately wanted to start a family) and both partners were financially independent, so there was very little holding her back.

Other, that is, than her values.

She was a face-to-face client and when we went through The Clarity Method™ and I showed her the results, we both started laughing. She had a number-one core value of Freedom, which was something she obviously wasn't getting from her marriage. She felt trapped by her environment and yearned to break free.

Unfortunately, her number-one anti-value was Conflict, and she knew perfectly well that a break-up of the marriage would have to cause some conflict, especially with his family with whom she was very close and didn't want to fall out with.

Uncovering a massive conflict like this doesn't necessarily make it go away. However, it does make it exponentially easier to deal with. It's very difficult solving a problem when you don't even know it exists. Having a certain sense of unease stopping you from doing something is not the same as being able to say, "Oh, I know what that is; it's just a value conflict and I can deal with it."

Donna and I spent another session discussing ways she could limit and deal with the conflict in the breakup whilst still allowing herself to move toward freedom.

The irony is that when she finally made the jump, the conflict she had envisaged never even materialized. The breakup was very good-natured and her relationship with her husband's family remained intact and amicable.

DMITRI—TYPE 3

Dmitri was very much a family guy. He had moved to the US from Russia with his parents and three older siblings when he was only two years old. Thirty years on, he still lived within an hour's drive of all but one of his siblings and his parents.

He had two kids of his own and the entire family would make a point of getting together on a regular basis. Family really did come first for him and it was no surprise that they were his number-one value.

Number two on Dmitri's list was Freedom and for him this was very much about financial freedom. Even though he'd had a trauma-free and relatively happy upbringing, his parents were quite poor. As such and being the youngest of four, as a kid his wardrobe was full of hand-me-downs. He never even got to play video games prior to his taking a part-time job and earning the money himself. And, for the first 16 years of his life, he'd never had the luxury of having his own bedroom.

When it came to going to college, his parents had no money and he didn't have a scholarship, so he spent four years working like a Trojan doing school work whilst delivering pizzas and working behind a bar.

Understandably, he wanted it to be different for his kids, and that meant earning a decent income so he could save to put them through college. The only problem was that in his current job the only way to earn the kind of money he wanted was to work weekends.

This is a classic Type 3 internal value conflict.

You can look at the example above and think, "Well that's so obvious that's going to cause trouble at some stage down the line because something has to give." You'd be right, but a great many people don't see this staring them in the face when their focus is elsewhere.

Your job as a coach or manager is to help people expand their focus and see what that brings. If people are still intent on heading off down the same path thinking that things will change in the future, then that is their choice. They are in all probability wrong, but sometimes we have to make our own mistakes rather than have somebody else advise that they are looming.

"Leaders honor their core values, but they are flexible in how they execute them."

—Colin Powell, four-star general and former Secretary of State

12

Using The Clarity Method™ to Motivate Client Action

If you have done The Clarity Method™ properly, you are now part of a tiny group of people wandering around this planet who actually know the hierarchy of their values and what makes them tick. You also have a clearer idea of why (and just as importantly, where) there may be sticking points in your life and the lives of the people you are coaching.

That in and of itself is incredibly useful, but there's much more.

You may well have heard of the neuro-linguistic programming (NLP) pain and pleasure model, based on the work of 18th-century English philosopher Jeremy Bentham. This model suggests that every human behavior is either designed to move away from pain or toward pleasure.

The pain and pleasure model (also called the towards-away from model) works at the macro level, but also at the micro level. And when I say every single human behavior or action is designed to provide pleasure or avoid pain, I do mean every single one; there are no exceptions. Even something as benign as rolling over to catch an extra 10 minutes' sleep in the morning could be classed as either a desire for pleasure (napping) or the desire to avoid pain (leaving a warm snuggly bed on a cold winter's morning).

If you took a close look at all the decisions you make on a moment-by-moment basis (although I wouldn't advise this because you make literally thousands per day and most are at an unconscious level), you would start to get a feel for whether you are predominantly deciding to do things to gain pleasure or to avoid pain.

There is a reasonable chance that the people you are using The Clarity Method™ with will find one side of the values process easier to do than the other. Maybe they skated through the anti-values but got bogged down with the core values, or vice versa.

This is going to give you a strong indication as to whether they are primarily motivated by moving toward things they want, or away from things they don't want. As a coach or manager, this knowledge can be incredibly useful, especially when dealing with clients who have motivation and procrastination issues.

Even though my aforementioned time at Yell was less than optimal, I did have the pleasure of working under the best manager of my career. The first time I met Nic Eatch was shortly before he had even accepted the position, when he invited me into an empty side office for a chat.

I sat down and he followed me in and immediately asked if I wanted a coffee. When I said yes, he didn't call for somebody else to bring me one but went and fetched it himself.

He came back into the office, shut the door, and handed me the hot coffee and sat on the edge of the desk grinning at me. "Now then, Tim," he said, "how do you like to be managed?"

I nearly fell off my chair. In 15 years of sales, nobody had asked me how I liked to be managed before. They pretty much did what they wanted to do and hoped it worked. If his reputation as a great guy and world-class salesperson hadn't preceded him, I'd have presumed I was being set up for some kind of gag.

Nic soon got to know that I was more of an 'away from' person. Sure, I liked hitting targets and earning bonuses, but not as much as I hated ever being near the bottom of a sales table.

Of course, the net result is exactly the same, but he figured out very quickly what was most likely to motivate me.

He also took the trouble to ask me values-based questions and to really get to know me as a person and what I was likely to be motivated and demotivated by. He never called me when I was at home because he knew I didn't like that, and he would actually gently reprimand me if I emailed him out of office hours. On one occasion he responded immediately saying, "Shouldn't you be spending time with your lovely wife rather than emailing me?"

And he did that with every member of our team to such an amazing extent that under his guidance we shattered just about every Yell sales record there was on the following campaign. In fact, we did this to such an extent that we forced a multibillion-dollar company to review and change its commission structure because we earned so much in bonuses.

Yes, there were some very talented salespeople in our close-knit team, but it was Nic's attention to detail when it came to understanding us individually that had us motivated and prepared to walk through walls for him.

Are you a toward or an away-from person?

Before you answer that question, let me offer a small piece of advice. It seems to me that on the whole, people prefer to think of themselves as being motivated by what they want rather than what they don't want. Many in the self-development industry continually batter home the message that we should all be super positive all the time when life just isn't like that—at least not for most people.

It really doesn't matter what motivates you as long as you know what it is and can harness it. It is what it is and there are no more kudos or Brownie points attached to being a toward person than an away-from person. Accept that you are what you are, and use it to your advantage rather than trying to be something you're not. Also, accept what others are too, because trying to change people at that level is a fool's errand and never going to work.

It is our job when working with others to step into their map of the world and not to try and get them to use ours.

By and large, we are programmed to be more aware of danger than we are reward. Evolutionarily this makes perfect sense: ignoring that snapping twig behind you may mean you're lunch for the saber-toothed tiger, whereas not catching that buffalo just means you go hungry for a bit longer.

For many people, negative motivation can be equally or even more powerful than positive motivation. As coaches, we should not limit the number of tools we have at our disposal by always framing things in a positive manner if that is not what a client responds best to.

Note: There is another type of negative motivation that is popular—if all the memes on Pinterest are anything to go by—but seldom useful. Using the desire to prove others wrong or seek revenge is sometimes okay in short bursts but it's limited as a long-term motivational strategy.

First, it's emotionally tiring and unsustainable for any length of time. But second, and more important, it seldom leads to anything other than short-term satisfaction. The best motivation comes from an internal locus of control. In other words, it is driven by your core values, what you truly want, and is not dictated by outside influence.

If your self-worth and happiness are dependent on what other people think of you or your accomplishments, then you're in for a rocky ride because you're never in control of your own life. And do you already know what is at the root of ALL stress?

Yep, you've remembered correctly, a lack of control.

I've noticed over the years that when a client has struggled with one side of the The Clarity Method™ and not the other, they nearly always turned out to favor the easy side as their primary motivation.

If both sides of the equation were equally easy (or difficult), it may well be they are sat closer to the middle, and their motivation will vary depending on the context and task at hand—and that is absolutely fine, too.

If your client is a strongly away-from person, how useful do you think it is going to be if you help her set goals that promise untold love, glory, and riches months or even years down the road?

Probably not very useful.

No matter how much you get her to think of her overflowing bank balance or stare at her vision board with its beautiful house and shiny new car, it's probably not going to inspire her other than at a very superficial level. And it certainly won't have her bouncing out of bed at 5am to scrape ice off her windshield so she can drive 200 miles to an important meeting.

I know this is going very much against conventional wisdom even with some of my peers but in my opinion, you'd be much better served to think about what she doesn't want—because that's what is going to get her fired up.

The thought of a pink slip from her job, a notice of intent to disconnect the electricity, or a letter from a potential book publisher telling her, "It appears your eight-year-old child sent us her school project by mistake," is much more likely to get her motivated and itching to take action.

Similarly, if she's a strongly toward person and she wants to quit smoking, then forget about suggesting she look at photos of diseased lungs, yellow fingers, and imagining her untimely demise. Instead, have her visualize a brilliant future in perfect health playing with her grandkids or even running a marathon at age 70.

I'm not saying that somebody who tends to be an away-from person will never be motivated toward things or vice versa, because there will be shifts depending on the context.

As I mentioned, I was never really motivated by big bonuses when I was working in sales. That is, until I was within touching distance of a monster payout. Then I turned into a drooling whirling dervish of sales-related activity intent on squeezing every last bit of bonus I could.

Of course, the net result is the same; the further I moved away from the bottom of a sales table, by default the closer I moved toward the top. However, knowing where to keep your clients' focus is the crucial thing to maximizing their potential and minimizing the chances of procrastination.

If you can nail down where your clients' motivation lies and focus on that as much as you can, then you are exponentially less likely to see their enthusiasm dip and see them start to procrastinate on projects. As a coach, the single most difficult issue to deal with is procrastinating clients. Very broadly speaking, since there are dozens of nuances, people procrastinate because their focus is in the wrong place and not because they are lazy or stupid.

Note: A few years ago, I read *Solving the Procrastination Puzzle: A Concise Guide to Strategies for Change* by Timothy A. Pychyl, PhD. Pychyl is probably the world's leading expert on procrastination and I really admire his work. Not only was the book excellent but I was beaming like a demented Cheshire cat when I got to the part where he was extolling the benefits of knowing your core values when it comes to beating procrastination. If the good doctor says so, then that's good enough for me!

You may come up with other reasons why clients procrastinate, such as a sense of overwhelm, a lack of information, or a lack of motivation. In the end, they all stem from of a lack of focus, or more accurately, a lack of focus in the right area.

Overwhelm is frequently caused by focusing on the big picture rather than on the next task. A lack of information is because the person isn't focusing on how to acquire that information.

Leaving depression to one side, a lack of motivation is often caused by people focusing on the pain of a task or change rather than the benefits.

Note: If you have a client who does the core values easily and struggled with the anti-values and insists she is not a toward person at all, and it's stuff she wants to avoid that gets her moving (or, vice versa, nailed the anti-values but wrestled with the core values but claims to not be an away-from person), then take that into account.

I have had the occasional client who has bucked the trend, and that's absolutely fine. This isn't an exact science. However, as I mentioned above, some people don't like the idea of thinking they are an away-from person and may insist they are motivated more by achievement.

In situations like this I would agree with the client (it's never our job to tell them they're wrong) but also be on the lookout for behaviors that tell me even though she thinks that, something altogether different is happening under the surface.

Another note: As I mentioned above, you may be somebody who is closer to the middle of the scale and your motivation varies depending on context. If that is the case, up your odds of getting pumped by looking at both what you want and what you don't want at the same time.

"Core values and culture are the only common thread for a company that can ensure that people with different education, upbringing, training, exposure, personality, gender or race can work for common goals."

—*Sandeep Aggarwal, founder of Droom*

13

How Do We Help Others Apply This Information?

I had a really interesting conversation with a client shortly after the first version of this book was published. We had spent some time working through The Clarity Method™ and she wanted to know how to best apply the information that we had uncovered to improve the quality of her life.

That sounds like a really obvious question but it's one I'd never been asked before. It had me wondering if other clients had thought the same thing but didn't like to ask. I had obviously made the mistake of thinking the application was obvious, when apparently it wasn't. So this brings us to Phase 3: Values Application.

Every time I take on a new client, I always kick things off by telling them they are free to challenge me. If they think I'm wrong on something, I want them to tell me because it means one of two things: either I am wrong, in which case we need to correct it. Or, I hadn't explained myself clearly enough and I needed to take more time to do so. In either situation, it's on me, not the client.

The client in question seemed to think that knowing her core values was merely useful in retrospect—that the main value was that she could look back on an event such as an internal meeting at work and realize after the fact why it didn't go as well as she'd liked by studying her values.

And that's true, she could do that, because most disagreements will come down to values if you dig deep enough.

However, there are other ways for your clients to use their values to improve the quality of their life and raise their happiness levels, other than merely analyzing something that didn't go as planned after the event.

Sometimes we can use them proactively (such as in decision making), sometimes they are ingrained and happen naturally, and other times (like in the above example) we can use them retrospectively.

And therein lies the beauty and the importance of understanding values—because they are constantly impacting everything we do and say, whether it's at a conscious or an unconscious level.

To give you an idea of what I mean, I'm going to use myself as an example. I'll run through four of my top eight values—in no particular order, along with some supporting case studies—and explain what the words mean to me and how I use them to my benefit, and in what context. As we spoke about previously, you could have very different meanings and that's fine.

PEACE

When I refer to peace, I am always meaning peace of mind. World peace is nice and I'm all for it but at this stage in our evolutionary development, it's probably not a reality outside of a beauty pageant contestant's head.

However, peace of mind can always be a reality no matter the external circumstances. If, that is, you work at it and really persevere, and then work and really persevere some more.

There are several reasons I meditate but none are more important than trying to cultivate equanimity and inner peace.

People sometimes confuse equanimity with apathy when they are in no way connected.

Equanimity allows you to retain your own personal power because you decide to react with calm no matter how trying the circumstances.

It doesn't mean you'll never be sad or that you'll be in a permanent state of bliss, it just means you won't spend your entire life mindlessly reacting to situations, many of which aren't even within your control.

Is this ingrained for me or does it need work?

For me it most definitely requires a lot of work, and it's work that will never end. I definitely tend to become defensive and grumpy if things aren't going my way. I am also very easily sucked into petty arguments on social media—usually on matters political—but meditation is helping me improve that aspect of my personality.

How can I use this to be happier?

Apart from the fact that meditation itself has been proven to increase happiness levels, the sheer fact that I'm less likely to get down under certain circumstances by default means I'm living a happier life.

INTEGRITY

Probably the single biggest reason I left sales was because I was regularly asked to do things that, in my opinion, lacked integrity.

As a coach and leader, if I don't act with integrity then I'm dead in the water because (hopefully) nobody in their right mind would hire a coach who lacks integrity.

When I offered almost $1,000 worth of free coaching to somebody if I failed to go the month of November in 2012 without alcohol, it would have been easy for me to have lied and not admitted to crumbling in the face of a very sexy pinot noir on Thanksgiving.

That would indeed have saved me some time, and nobody would have ever known. Except that is, me, and I would have been extremely irritated with myself.

Ingrained or needs work?

For me, thanks to my dad, this is largely ingrained. I'm not saying I never have to take a step back and remind myself, but it's not something that I am actively working on like peace of mind.

How can I use this to be happier?

Integrity is vitally important to me and if I constantly act in ways that breach that value I will, over time, give my self-esteem a good kicking.

It may seem weird and woo-woo, but I feel lighter and more at ease when I know I'm acting with integrity. It didn't bother me to give the free life coaching away because the alternative was much worse.

FREEDOM

For me, freedom is really about freedom to do what I want, when I want. Now, I do understand that's not always possible but by and large (and finances notwithstanding) I have pretty much nailed this aspect since becoming a life coach.

Ingrained or needs work?

I think this is largely ingrained for me. If I get a request for coaching midweek at 11:00am, I automatically say no because that's when I take my dogs out, and nobody messes with my dog-walking!

I also get to decide when I take time off, which clients I say yes to, and when I want to post a blog. Unfortunately, I don't get to decide on whether I empty the dishwasher or what to watch on TV, so I'm not totally there yet.

How can I use this to be happier?

As I have already said, the two biggest stressors in people's lives are lack of choice and lack of autonomy, resulting in a lack of control. My definition of freedom gives me choice the vast majority of the time, and because I am working for myself, I always have complete autonomy.

Therefore, as stress and happiness are almost mutually exclusive, it gives me a great deal of control in my life and increases the likelihood of being happier.

CASE STUDY: MEET RYAN

Ryan was the CFO and majority owner of a very successful high-tech family-owned and -operated business in California. He had moved to Florida the previous year after he sold the company to an Orlando-based business for several million dollars.

Part of the deal was that he stayed in place as chief financial officer for two years to oversee the segue, reassure customers that they would receive the same high level of service, and hold the hand of the people taking over.

He only had a few months to go and as he was only in his late forties, he was getting anxious about what he was going to do thereafter.

With his qualifications and experience, he knew he would have no problem getting another job as a CFO in a medium-sized organization, albeit probably not close by. However, there were two stumbling blocks to that.

First, he had two boys in school, and he didn't want to move them because they were happy and at the age where a major disruption may negatively impact their academic success.

Second, prior to selling the business, he had spent the vast majority of his adult life effectively working for himself, and he liked it that way. The previous 18 months or so had been tough on him with lots of empire building and office politics to contend with. It reminded him of how important it was for him to have not just financial freedom, but the freedom to work where and when he wanted and with whom.

He had signed a five-year non-compete clause forbidding him from working within the same sector as he had come from in the state of Florida, but in any case, he really wanted a change and to buy a completely different business.

He had been trawling the listings of going concerns that were for sale and getting despondent because he didn't know anything about the different industries.

We had done The Clarity Method™ exercise and amongst his top values were, Family, Freedom, Giving Back, and Fun.

We talked about some of the companies that were available and for each one he pointed out his lack of experience in that particular sector and how he found that demotivating.

I asked him if he thought Warren Buffett knew the minutiae of every business he bought. This created a small shift when he replied, "Of course not."

I followed that up by asking that if he was the CFO of a business, would he need to know the intricacies of the industry when presumably he would hire a manager or a chief operating officer who had expertise and experience in that field? Again, he answered that he wouldn't.

On the intake call, he had told me of his respect for Howard Schultz, the CEO of Starbucks. Schultz was born into a poor family in Brooklyn, New York. When his father, a truck driver barely making ends meet, broke his ankle, things deteriorated quickly.

His father didn't have medical insurance and as he couldn't work, the forced time off caused a great deal of heartache and hardship to their family.

Those memories remained with Schultz all his life and when he bought Starbucks in 1988, he insisted that every employee receive full medical benefits. That was relatively easy for him as he was the owner.

Nevertheless, by the time Schultz returned as CEO after an eight-year hiatus in 2008, he took his commitment to his employees a stage further. The company was in serious financial difficulty, as were many businesses at that time. But Starbucks was spending more on employee healthcare than it was on coffee.

Shareholders were calling to scrap the health benefits, but Schultz pushed back hard and refused to revoke even part-time employee healthcare rights. A greater example of refusing to compromise on your values is hard to imagine and I could understand why Ryan had so much respect for him.

Ryan, too, had been passionate about looking after the people who worked for him and even though he didn't have to, he made sure that every single one was generously remunerated when the business was sold.

It would be easy to see a value like Giving Back and presume it has charitable connotations. Of course, that will often be the case, but for Ryan it meant creating a business that offered good wages, a safe environment, and support in whatever shape was needed for his employees.

I suggested we take another look at some of the business opportunities he had and instead of looking at them the traditional way, we look at them through the lens of his values.

Which of them allowed him to work from home if he wanted, to put his family first, to have fun, and to give back?

This shifted his perspective entirely and he visibly perked up and became more engaged and enthused.

Even I was surprised when he decided he wanted to research a landscaping company. That was until he told me he used to work for his uncle's lawn care company during the summers when he was still in school and loved it.

A few months later, Ryan was the owner of his own small landscaping company. It wasn't the original one he had seen, as that didn't quite meet his requirements, but one he had hired to do some work on his own lawn.

I'm sure that if we had maintained the same way of looking at his situation, we would have struggled to get past the impasse traditional thinking can create.

Knowing his core values gave Ryan the clarity he needed to move forward, confident that he was making the correct decision even though on the surface it seemed like a strange career detour.

TOLERANCE

There's nothing that bugs me more than intolerant people, which is possibly hypocritical because that means I'm intolerant of intolerance!

If you're reading this book, I don't care if you're a Muslim or a Jew, if you're black or white, gay or straight, Republican or Democrat, or Crip or Blood, because you're obviously trying to work on yourself and improve your lot in life.

Life ain't easy and I respect anybody who is trying to become a better person.

Ingrained or needs work?

Yikes, this definitely needs work, because as I already said I can be brutally intolerant toward people, organizations, religions, and cultures that persecute and ostracize people because they're different.

How can I use this to be happier?

This is more abstract and has less impact on my happiness levels than the other values listed. However, whenever I can demonstrate tolerance—and also compassion, which often flows out of tolerance—I do feel happier and better about myself.

CASE STUDY: MEET JENNIFER

When Jennifer came to see me, she was about to start her second year of law school. She was married with an eight-year-old son, and her husband had a well-paid corporate job that required him to travel extensively.

Prior to deciding to go to law school, she had been a very successful salesperson and earned a six-figure salary but had become burned out by the long hours and increasing stress levels.

As her son was now at school and she'd had an interest in law for as long as she could remember, she decided to go back to school to become an attorney.

Unfortunately, she had struggled in the first year and was finding the workload much greater than she anticipated and wanted help dealing with the stress she was under.

Any alarm bells ringing yet?

When Jennifer sent her values to me before we went through the ordering process, I was stunned. Three of the anti-values on her list were Confrontation, Stress, and Anxiety.

I have never worked in law, although I have worked with a few attorneys. I don't need to be John Grisham to realize the legal profession, for the most part, is a high-stress, high-conflict industry.

As per how I operate, I didn't say anything to Jennifer prior to taking her through The Clarity Method™. I merely went through the list to get an understanding of what she meant by each word and to make sure I didn't impose my interpretations on her values.

What discomfort I had was magnified tenfold by the time we had finished the process, because her anti-values list had Conflict at the top and Stress at number two.

As I wrote her values on the whiteboard for her to take a look at, I waited for the penny to drop. She looked at them but didn't say anything. She just nodded appreciatively and kept her focus on her core values and away from the anti-values.

I asked her if anything stood out, or if they were pretty much as she expected. She shrugged her shoulders and muttered that they were what she would have expected.

It's important to explain at this stage that I was frustrated as hell—because, as you know, it is not the role of a coach to tell our clients what to do. Our job is to ask the right questions and hope that they will come to the best conclusions available to them.

I say that because this is one occasion on which I badly wanted to scream, "You're training for the wrong job, woman, and no amount of stress management or tips and tricks will alter that fact"—but unfortunately, I couldn't.

Yet another cognitive bias had come into play here and this time it is was the sunk-cost fallacy.

If you have ever remained in a relationship that you knew in your heart of hearts was doomed, or if you ever carried on repairing a car that you knew was beyond the pale—or even if you have ever refused to sell an item you possess for a fair market value simply because you paid more for it—then you have been the victim of sunk-cost fallacy.

When we have invested time, money, emotion, or a combination of all three in something that we know isn't working, it's very difficult for our brain to allow us to walk away. To do so means accepting it was a mistake to not walk away sooner, and that rascal of a brain will rebel against that with all its might.

Jennifer had poured a lot of time and money into her first year of law school. On top of that, she was incredibly and emotionally invested in the idea of being a criminal lawyer. Her brain was playing every card it had available to make sure she didn't backtrack on her sunk cost.

I started to realize she hadn't hired me to get a clearer understanding of whether her chosen career was the right one for her. She had hired me to help her confirm to herself that she had made a good decision to continue with law school even though all the signs said otherwise.

Deep down, I have absolutely no doubt she knew she was on the wrong career path but admitting that to herself would have created so much cognitive dissonance that it was easier to simply shut down and not accept it than to deal with the consequences.

I would love to tell you that I asked Jennifer one mind-blowing question that allowed her to see the error she was about to make and that she dropped out of law school, but it didn't pan out like that.

We did work together for a couple of sessions more, but nothing I did could get her to re-evaluate her situation. I even went as far as asking her if she thought there was a potential conflict looming whilst pointing to the anti-values. She responded that she thought she could deal with it, especially if I could show her some relaxation and stress management techniques.

Don't get me wrong; stress management and relaxation techniques are great but they're not as great as not needing them in the first place. Jennifer was in a situation that we have all been in at times, and that is she was looking to confirm a decision she had already made.

Sometimes as coaches we have to accept that our hands are tied, and we cannot help every client who comes to us.

"So, when these people sell out, even though they get fabulously rich, they're gypping themselves out of one of the potentially most rewarding experiences of their unfolding lives. Without it, they may never know their values or how to keep their newfound wealth in perspective."

—Steve Jobs, co-founder of Apple Inc.

14

Inherent Values

This is by far the most difficult chapter for me to write because even in my own mind I vacillate on what to do with the information I am about to share with you. In fact, I may bring it up with one client and not even mention it with the next, depending on my gut instinct and the results I gain, rather than any golden rule.

In the original incarnation of this book, called *Aligning With Your Core Values*, I referred to inherent values as meta-values and described them as values that sit above all other values. Over the last few years, I have shifted my stance somewhat and, with the one exception of happiness, no longer think of these values as being necessarily more important than any others at an individual level.

The reason I want to talk with you about what I now prefer to think of as *inherent* values is because they are easy for clients to take for granted or forget about, and thus you are left not knowing the full picture.

The best way to see what I mean with this is to compare the four inherent values I highlight on the following pages against the values you have on your own list, one by one.

Presuming the inherent value isn't on your list already, merely compare it to what is at number eight and ask yourself if that inherent value is more important to you than your number-eight value. If the answer is no, then you are good to go, and you can move on to the next one.

If, on the other hand, the answer is yes, then compare it to the value at number seven. Keep doing that, working your way up the list, until you find out where it slots.

And just in case you're wondering, priming is again the reason I didn't mention inherent values beforehand. If I had done that, there would have been a good chance I could have influenced the results of your value elicitation. That's also the reason why I never mention them to clients.

HAPPINESS

I'm not a soothsayer, clairvoyant, or mind reader, but I do know without question one thing about you. You want to be happy, and so will every person you ever meet. The reason I know this is because you're a human being and every human being strives to be happy.

You may think you know miserable people who don't enjoy being happy, but you'd be wrong. Either they are adopting a strategy for happiness that isn't working, or they don't believe happiness is an option and as such prefer not to seek it, and instead, feel let down.

The human brain will do all sorts of weird and wonderful things to avoid disappointment rather remarkably, including making itself disappointed. When you meet people like this, always call to mind the NLP (neuro-linguistic programming) presupposition that every action has a positive intention. There is literally

NOTHING that you or anybody else does that doesn't have a positive intent underlying it.

We may look back on certain behaviors with hindsight and think they were stupid or ill-advised bearing in mind the outcome, but at the time, we were seeking a positive outcome. Even extreme actions like self-harm and suicide are driven by a positive intention, such as a cry for help or gaining an endorphin rush in the former or seeking peace or not wanting to be a burden to others with the latter.

This is the exception when I said I didn't necessarily mean inherent values sit *above* all other values, just that all people have them—because I strongly believe that happiness is everybody's number-one value.

Presuming you didn't have happiness at number one, ask yourself the reason you want all your other values. Look at your list and then ponder how you will feel if you are in alignment with all your top eight values. Happy, right?

When I get a client with happiness on his or her list, I dismiss it and will often ask them to give me another one. Knowing clients want to be happy tells me absolutely nothing about them, and it doesn't help me coach them.

FAIRNESS

There are certain emotions that are hard-wired into us, and fairness is one of them. It's the reason that people can act so irrationally and emotionally when they think they have been treated unfairly.

There was a famous experiment conducted that beautifully epitomizes our desire for fairness and how that desire can make us act in ways that make little or no sense.

Two people who didn't know each other were placed in separate rooms. One person was given $10 and told he or she had to decide how much to keep and how much to give the other person. The other person could then either accept or reject the offer. If he or she chose to reject it, however, neither person got any money.

Interestingly, people were more likely to offer a split close to 50/50 than you might imagine. Not unsurprisingly, when offered half or close to half of the amount, the other person almost always accepted.

However, the twist came with the people who decided they wanted more than 50%. When offers of $8 to $2 and even $7 to $3 were made, the potential recipients of the lower amount frequently rejected the bid and both people ended up with nothing.

Logically, this makes no sense. Remember—they didn't know the other person and they were being offered an amount of money for doing nothing, so why on earth would they turn it down?

It was because they felt it wasn't equitable and they would rather cut their nose off to spite their face than let the other person treat them in an unfair manner.

If you have ever found yourself counting the items in the basket of the person in front of you whilst standing in the '10 items or less' line and then going postal when you realized the old lady had 12, you have experienced the power of fairness.

I have used this idea many times with clients to remarkable effect. Often, they will really value fairness (justice, kindness, and compassion can be used in the same way) and yet still be tough on themselves.

I will merely ask them this question: "If you really value fairness, should you not extend that fairness to yourself and not be beating yourself up repeatedly for past mistakes or indiscretions?"

LOVE/CONNECTION

You may be a macho male ripped like a side of beef and have more testosterone coursing through your veins than a major league baseball team, but you still need love and connection to and from other human beings.

The Beatles may have got it slightly wrong by saying love is all you need, but it is definitely a *need* and not a want. There's a good reason why solitary confinement is considered such a severe form of punishment in prisons the world over—because it messes with our heads.

A huge unplanned human experiment was conducted in Romania in the 1980s under the brutal regime of Nicolae Ceausescu. Although the results provided an invaluable insight into the human psyche and our need for love and connection (especially in our developmental stages), this knowledge was attained at the cost of terrible human suffering.

Under Ceausescu, birth control was illegal, and the country was suffering terrible poverty and food shortages. Many families simply couldn't afford to bring children into the world as they were already living in abject poverty and struggling to put food on the table.

In a move of breathtaking stupidity and callousness, the Romanian government gave families the option to give up their kids to state-run orphanages. Sadly, many thousands of families took up this option, no doubt brainwashed to a certain extent into believing the government could do a better job of raising their kids.

While in the orphanages, the kids had little contact with adults—and what contact they did have was not the kind that children yearn for. In fact, it was often nothing short of barbaric.

In other words, they got no love and no meaningful connection either physically or psychologically.

There have been various scientific studies done on these children since then, and none of the results make for pleasant reading. This isn't the book to go into those details. You can Google it if you want to learn more, although it won't cheer you up and I'm not sure there's much benefit to reading about it. Suffice to say, on the whole, the kids did not exactly flourish.

They were far more likely to have learning difficulties, struggle to form relationships, and have antisocial behavioral issues later on in life.

I don't care how self-reliant you are or how much you like your peace and quiet, but you still need human interaction in some way, shape, or form if you want to maintain your sanity, especially when you are growing up.

This value is a trickier one to apply with a client, especially Type-A guys who may wince at the thought of feeling they need to connect, or that love is important to their happiness. But there have been a few occasions where I've had a client who gave every signal that this was important to them, and in such cases, it's our job to maybe probe a bit more and challenge our clients.

Note: If you have read *Walden* by Henry David Thoreau, then you may be considering firing off an email to me telling me how he spent two years alone and still managed to knock out a classic book, but there are three important things to take into consideration.

First, Thoreau did have occasional contact with the outside world when absolutely necessary.

Second, and more important, he chose a solitary existence. It wasn't imposed upon him like the aforementioned solitary confinement that has been known to send people insane. Thoreau always had the ability to quit his lifestyle and return to his previous existence.

And third, Thoreau was a well-developed adult man and his brain wasn't still in the process of maturing and developing neural connections.

HEALTH

I thought long and hard before I finally decided to place Health in my Inherent Value list. And the reason I thought about it so long is because I know a lot of sick people who are happy, and a helluva lot of healthy people who are deeply unhappy.

However, just because we can be sick and still remain optimistic and even happy, that is not the same as saying at least a measure of good health isn't incredibly important to every single person.

When we are young, unless we have health problems, being fit and well tends to be something we take for granted. But as we age, we realize that it's not the given that we always presumed it would be.

I have a condition called hemochromatosis, which basically means I have too much iron in my blood. So yes, indeed, you can call me 'Man of Iron' and not be exaggerating. The treatment necessitates having a phlebotomy to drain off a pint of blood once a month to keep the ferritin in my blood down to safe levels.

Because I am under the care of a hematologist, I have my phlebotomies on an oncology ward alongside cancer patients having chemotherapy treatment. And I often see more smiles on that ward in an hour or so than I do for the rest of the day combined.

I think that is a massive testament to the human spirit and demonstrates perfectly that we can be happy even under the most adverse of conditions.

Still, even though that is possible, I believe that most people deeply desire good health above many other things, even if sometimes that's not obvious by their behaviors. When I gave Health as an example of a value that can come from nowhere to the top of somebody's list based on a health scare, what I really meant was that their value of health was exposed. It was always really there.

If you are looking to help clients break negative and harmful patterns of behavior such as overeating, smoking, etc., dig a little deeper if they don't have health on their list. It may be more a question of denial on their part. If they don't see it down there, then they don't have to align with it.

As I was writing *The Clarity Method*, I had an interesting experience with a client.

We had gone through the process and come up with a list of values that she was very happy with and was certain represented her. I was puzzled because nowhere on her list was the value of Family. This isn't that unusual as I frequently work with people who have no close family, don't particularly like their family, or are estranged from them, and as such it doesn't make the list.

This woman wasn't like that, though. She was very happily married, had a daughter on the way, and was also very close with her parents.

In situations like this, do not be afraid to challenge your clients. An easy way to do it is like this. After I had the completed lists, I looked at the bottom value on her list which happened to be

Creativity and asked her, "What's more important to you, Creativity or Family?"

She looked at me like I had asked her if she preferred live aardvark on toast or pancakes for breakfast and said, "Why family, of course."

I then asked her the same question with the value that was at number seven, and we worked the way up the list until it slotted in at number two.

As I say, never be afraid to challenge your clients in this manner because sometimes things are so obvious to people, they forget. This client was a tad embarrassed when we finally found Family's correct place in the list, but she really didn't need to be because it's very easy to miss that which is closest to us.

Warning: Never ask a client *before* you have completed The Clarity Method™ with about why a value you know to be important to them isn't on their values list. If you do, you once again risk the dreaded 'priming' and also having them give you the answer they think you want to hear.

"It's not hard to make decisions when you know what your values are."

—Roy E. Disney, co-founder of Walt Disney Productions

15

Values That Aren't Really Values

I want to throw some words at you now and explain why I don't really consider them to be values. You may disagree, and as a coach you may or may not want to have them on a client's list. In either case, they still give you valuable information as to what makes a client tick.

MONEY

I wish I had $100 for every client who tried to tell me money was a value of theirs and to whom I have had to patiently explain that it wasn't. If I did, I'd quite possibly be lying on a beach in Bali now and not writing *The Clarity Method*. (Or better still, I'd be writing *The Clarity Method* whilst lying on a beach in Bali.)

I'm sure you would like some more money—most people would—but I'm equally sure you want some more to spend, donate to a good cause, or invest, not to stare at. Money can only ever be a means to an end; it's not the end in itself.

I would like some more money to allow me to travel far more extensively and take more regular trips back to the UK to see friends and family. Therefore, if I use myself as an example, it's quite obvious that I see money as a means to more Freedom or even Connection.

Equally, I would like to do more mentoring and coaching for people who can't afford my services but would benefit substantially.

I was recently blown away to read that world-renowned coach Marshall Goldsmith was going to take on not just one coach to mentor, or even three or four, but 100. Yes, he was making himself available to 100 people, many of whom were already very accomplished coaches, to help take them to the next level.

Do you think Marshall values Legacy and Significance? Do you think you'd need to do much digging to find out he wants to give back, pay it forward or whatever you want to call it, with the money he has acquired on the back of being a successful author and coach?

A decision like that, presuming there isn't some sinister motive, is always, and I do mean ALWAYS driven by values. But I'm pretty sure if Marshall had an empty bank account, four kids, and a huge mortgage to meet, then he wouldn't be making such an offer.

And that isn't in any way meant to diminish his gracious offer, but rather an observation that everything has to be a win-win if it is to remain sustainable.

Whereas money is never a value, it most definitely can help us tap into certain values and allow us to live them more fully without basic concerns like not being able to eat or shelter ourselves from the elements.

SECURITY AND/OR STABILITY

I've already addressed this thorny issue in some detail and explained why I'm dubious as to whether Security and Stability are genuine values. Of course, neither is sustainable but knowing that a client desires one or both strongly does give us insight into their thought process and what you are dealing with.

I will take either or both of these from a client, but I may then want to take the list down to 10 values to give me a better understanding of their needs. Both are likely to create internal value conflicts, so tread carefully.

DEATH

Even though Death is on my list of anti-values and clients will quite often choose it, I really do not consider it an anti-value, per se.

I want you to prepare yourself for some shocking and potentially life-changing news. Please sit down, have a stiff drink in hand (and maybe a portable defibrillator just in case), and take a deep breath before you move on.

You're going to die one day.

I'm sorry if that has come as a shock to you, and maybe you don't even believe me, but honestly, it's true. Google it if you're still doubtful.

You can speed up the process of death if you so wish. In fact, you could probably sample it today if you really wanted, although please don't. You may even be able to slow it down a tad by eating healthily, exercising, and not partaking in things that your body doesn't enjoy like smoking, drinking, and cage fighting.

But largely speaking, the biggest indicator of how long you will live is buried (pun intended) deep within your DNA and there is not much you can do about it.

Having said all that, death can be used as a motivator, especially when it's imminent. The blessing with death is also the problem. By and large, you have no idea when the fateful day will arrive, and therefore you can always put off doing meaningful work until another day.

In that respect, you can use death to motivate your clients. However, it's very tricky to do and you have to have built up a very high level of rapport because not many people like focusing on and thinking about their own mortality.

Death often must be imminent for it to truly motivate people, which is why we often see people who have been diagnosed with terminal illnesses doing amazing charitable work, mending broken relationships, or even finding inner peace. All of a sudden, they know for sure that time is running out more quickly than they anticipated, and they want to make what time they have left meaningful and worthwhile.

If you genuinely believe death can motivate you or the people you are taking through The Clarity Method™, then by all means use it. Just be aware you are rolling the dice and you could create the opposite effect, which is why I seldom focus on it.

"It's no good knowing your values if you don't live your values."

—Tim Brownson, some dude who wrote a book on values

You Did It! Well Done, You!

I know I joke around a lot. To me, life shouldn't be taken too seriously because as Jim Morrison from The Doors once said, "No one here gets out alive." And Jim should know; he's well and truly dead.

However, I do take my job very seriously (as I am sure you do), and I'm being honest when I say that with The Clarity Method™, you now have what I believe is the most important element in your armory as a coach or a leader at work.

I have no idea how coaches and leaders can maximize their effectiveness without doing values work with their clients and employees, yet many try. By reading this book and implementing the ideas herein, you have separated yourselves from those leaders and given yourself the opportunity to really help your clients and employees figure out what's going on in their lives.

I suggest that you run through The Clarity Method™ process from start to finish a couple of times on yourself to get comfortable with it. Then try it out on a few people before implementing it in your client work or with people in the workplace.

Even though it's not that complicated, it will take you a little while to get to the point where it flows smoothly for you—and you don't want to be stumbling over it with people you are looking to help, especially if they are paying you!

However, please don't try it out on family members or close friends. One of the cardinal sins of coaching is trying to coach people we know well. Why? Because we start to coach to our own agenda and not the client's. The less we know about a client prior to working with them, the better.

I wish you the best of luck—not just with using The Clarity Method™ values process but with your coaching techniques in general. As I write this, we all find ourselves in an industry that is highly competitive, and the best way we can separate ourselves from the competition is by doing all we can to make ourselves world-class.

Thanks for reading, best wishes, and if you have any comments, observations, or questions I can be reached at tim@theclaritymethod.com.

About the Author

Certified life coach and author Tim Brownson is known for his direct and honest approach to coaching clients to big breakthroughs. An in-demand coach, he is a Neuro-Linguistic Programming (NLP) Master Practitioner, Certified Hypnotherapist, internationally published author, and engaging public speaker.

Brownson has authored several books on personal development, including *70 Amazing Facts About Your Brain* and *Don't Ask Stupid Questions – There Are No Stupid Questions*. He is also co-author of *How To Be Rich and Happy* with John P. Strelecky.

Originally from the UK, Tim lives in Florida with his wife and dogs.

Remember to go to: www.claritymethod.com/bookstuff to watch the videos and download the forms.

Sample Core Values List

- Authenticity
- Bravery
- Commitment
- Community
- Connection
- Creativity
- Diversity
- Equality
- Fairness
- Family
- Freedom
- Fun
- Gratitude
- Growth
- Health
- Honesty
- Humility
- Humor
- Integrity
- Justice
- Kindness
- Knowledge
- Leadership
- Love
- Nurturing
- Open-mindedness
- Passion
- Patience
- Peace
- Persistence
- Positivity
- Prudence
- Security
- Self-control
- Service
- Significance
- Spirituality
- Stability
- Trust

Sample Anti-Values List

- Aggression
- Anger
- Anxiety
- Apathy
- Arrogance
- Betrayal
- Brutality
- Conflict
- Contempt
- Cynicism
- Death
- Disgust
- Dishonesty
- Fear
- Frivolity
- Greed
- Hate
- Hypocrisy
- Ill health
- Infidelity
- Immorality
- Injustice
- Isolation
- Jealousy
- Laziness
- Pain
- Pomposity
- Poverty
- Procrastination
- Stress
- Suspicion
- Worry

COPYRIGHT

Made in the USA
Columbia, SC
19 June 2019